LEARN, GROW, FORGIVE

A Path to Spiritual Success

Dr. Donna Marks

Learn, Grow, Forgive: A Path to Spiritual Success

Published by Westward Publishing
West Palm Beach, FL

First edition published by Balboa Press 2019

ISBN: 978-0-578-83158-9

SELF-HELP / Spiritual

Cover artwork by Mimie Langlois
Cover design by Grazie Prokopetz

Printed in the United States of America.

WESTWARD PUBLISHING

To Donna Bentolila, my analyst, who left this planet much too young, but not without giving new life to those of us she helped.

Some say life is hard, but for me, it was difficult only when I did not know what I was doing or how to do it.

Contents

PART III: FORGIVE

Acknowledgments

Special thanks to my husband, Skip, for many hours of reviewing this manuscript and providing his valuable input. His love and support are beyond description. I am also grateful to Julee Staley for her many hours of reading and discussion that helped to improve the contents and message of this book. I was fortunate to have some amazing artists who contributed to this book cover; Mimie Langlois for her artwork, Grazie Prokopetz for her graphic design, and A. Spencer Schwartz for his photography. I am also grateful to all of the people who brought me the painful challenges during my life so that I could learn, grow, and forgive.

Prologue

We are all meant to be happy. If things go well, a child comes into the world, receives sufficient emotional and physical nourishment, and develops into a well-adjusted person who finds a meaningful place in the world. This need not be first place or any particular place at all—only where the pleasures of life far exceed the inevitable challenges of life.

Many of us experienced a different reality. If things did not go well, our minds were unable to adapt to a nonsensical environment that felt scary and often empty. We might have looked outside ourselves to quiet the anxiety or enliven the deadness, a search that set the stage for dependence on things that offered quick, superficial fixes when emotionally overwhelmed.

What begins as an exciting experiment can quickly become an addiction, sucking away at our spiritual essence and replacing it with an ever-growing black hole. It leaves us free-floating in an abyss of pain, every ray of hope darkened by ominous clouds of disappointment and despair, tiny scraps of joy overshadowed by gloom, fatigue, and fear. Once the addiction has thoroughly hijacked the mind, death can descend slowly by eating away at one's physical being, or it may come quickly with unbearable and inescapable pain, often ending in suicide.

I was one of those who found themselves in the abyss of a senseless existence as pain screamed its way through every fiber of my being. After a seemingly endless stream of failed attempts to achieve the life I wanted, I finally cracked the code.

By the time I was thirty, I had hit an emotional bottom that set me on my path to mental and spiritual recovery. I joined a twelve-step program and found what I always missed at church: every walk of life, coming together to heal spiritually. Building on that foundation, I fully immersed myself in psychotherapy and a quest for truth. When a friend introduced me to *A Course in Miracles*, it felt like a warm fuzzy coat in freezing weather. It provided the connection I had been seeking my entire life and fed my soul with a sense of love and God. All of this opened a new door to personal development, spiritual growth, and a new beginning. I became free of chemical dependency and cigarettes, unloaded years of anger, and enjoyed professional success as a psychotherapist. I commenced to heal myself through every form of help I could find: Gestalt therapy, hypnosis, landmark education, psychodrama, and rational emotive therapy, to name a few. My spiritual search took me around the world, to Brazil, Peru, and Israel. I studied Buddhism, Christianity, Kabbalah, metaphysics, shamanism, and yoga. With all of this effort, however, I still magnetically attracted unhealthy relationships and failed at multiple marriages. My hardwired patterns seemed implacable. I found myself unable to align the disconnected parts of my mind that seemingly governed me. Even though I enjoyed professional success, a lingering sense of inauthenticity still haunted me; down deep, I felt like an unhealed healer.

My support system further reinforced my inner sense of deficiency. These people watched me wander in and out of failed relationships from which any sane person would have run. I dismissed or ignored those who dared to tell me the truth because—in my mind—they could not understand. Blinded by an unconscious past that overrode my internal navigation system, I was deaf to that ever-wise source I blamed for abandoning me along the way when in reality, it was I who stopped listening. My struggle with key relationships ultimately led me to give up and throw away my long-term sobriety. It felt like all of my efforts were for naught; I was baffled that I could not fix myself. Divorced with a child at age eighteen, I worked as a waitress while attending night school and then crawled my way out of poverty, one college degree at a time. I could not understand why the same rules for success would not apply to my personal life. *Where was the disconnect?* I obsessed without resolve. There would be many more failures before I was ready to face the parts of my mind that were unconsciously pulling my strings. I had to go deeper.

The breakthrough happened one day when I received a brochure at my office about psychoanalytic training and decided to check it out. Since Freud was a cocaine user, I had snubbed his work and never bothered to understand his vast contributions to psychology and psychoanalysis, from which all subsequent theories evolved. Desperate to change, I somehow intuitively knew that brochure represented newfound hope.

Psychoanalysis was an incredibly difficult process. It was like going into a dark cave with a dimming flashlight and waiting for the hidden monsters to emerge. Of course, the monsters were not real and were long gone, but their images disguised memories that I did not want to face. If I was going to make it out of the cave without imploding or running away, I needed a guide. My analyst was that person. She led me to understand the hidden part of my mind where those unconscious images were silently ruling my behavior.

As a child, I developed an anti-dependent attitude as a way of protecting myself from needing anyone or anything. By the time I was five, I had made a conscious effort to close down my heart as tightly as possible. Now, vulnerable and not in control, my anxiety caused me to fight the analysis every step of the way. Regardless, I continued the psychoanalytic work along with a twelve-step program.

My previous therapy never fully explored the emotional impact of my childhood trauma. Now in psychoanalysis, I had to face the emotional wreckage of my father, who I saw only two or three times after my parents were divorced. I had a stepfather I loved and trusted but who betrayed me with bouts of physical and verbal rage and often made sexual advances when he was drunk. I intuitively knew my stepfather was sick, and I felt sorry for him. I carried the burden of this secret trauma to protect my family from upheaval. In psychoanalysis, I had to face the impact these experiences had on me. I learned who I was in relationships with men—a broken girl who attracted men who reenacted that same betrayal.

Once I stopped resisting and opened up with my analyst, my heart began to thaw, and I started to grow. My tears streamed an unstoppable flow. I allowed my analyst's gentle voice to soothe me as I mourned the pain of those who had betrayed me. She helped me to understand the dynamics of a healthy relationship between a man and a woman and determine what was missing in my relationships. Slowly, a new image of a stable, emotionally healthy relationship replaced the long-held, defective model in my mind.

I continued to make mistakes, even foolish ones, but now there was someone to help me explore those life lessons and face the parts of me that were working against success. When I was scared and angry about doing the work, I recognized that my reactions were calling for healing and kept the commitment, no matter what. When I projected my past onto my therapist, she helped me to see that she was not one of the ghosts stored in the caverns of my mind. I learned to explore the roots of those feelings rather than acting out in self-defeating ways—like shutting down, self-medicating, or running away. Over time, I found myself able to have a healthy conversation with another person for the first time in my life—a relationship built on self-disclosure, honest feelings, and trust. As the old haunting voices in my head quieted, the channel to my inner spirit widened.

My grieving was complete when I forgave and then found gratitude for all of my past. Those experiences helped me to be a better therapist and gave me a depth of understanding that I didn't have before. I was able now to receive love and be the love I wanted—even toward those who had hurt me. Eventually, as a result of my core healing, the mental and spiritual dots connected. I no longer felt like a fraud. My spiritual quest began to make sense, and I could grasp the possibility of a pre-birth contract, an agreement to endure a challenging life for a higher purpose. Most importantly, I learned that spirituality is not just God and me; it meant loving myself and others, an impossibility without the deep healing my analysis provided. My life finally reflected my lifetime dreams and visions: the ability to be a better mother, a committed wife, and a true friend.

After navigating through my inner blockages, I could help others who also found themselves spinning their wheels.

Learn, Grow, Forgive, can change an insane mind-set from "doing the same thing over and over again and expecting different results" to new sanity: doing the same thing over and over again and getting different results. *Learn, Grow, Forgive* is a three-step process that will help you view mistakes as *learning* experiences rather than failures. You will stop judging setbacks, *grow* from those experiences, and *forgive* yourself too. You will feel inspired to shift your focus from hopeless, failed attempts to incremental successes and permanent change. The beautiful result of this process is self-love.

There is no magic fix for the pattern you are trying to break. The magic happens when you decide to choose loving actions rather than harmful behaviors. Some hard work will be required, and you will need to stay committed to the process, no matter how uncomfortable you feel. Right now, you can choose this journey out of your self-imprisoned maze into a life of intimacy and spiritual connectedness. The exercises in the following chapters outline a way to accelerate your healing. I share with you my more than thirty years of learning so that you can move at a faster pace. Once the clouds clear and the light shines through, the changes come fast. You need only accept that you are well worth the effort and decide that you can and will succeed. Never give up. Never, never, never.

Note: It is better that you do not rush through this work; take several days through each section to allow yourself to process and integrate what you are experiencing. If at any point the material feels overwhelming, consult a therapist.

Introduction

> The road to success and the road to failure
> are almost exactly the same.
> —Colin R. Davis

Nothing is ever hopeless unless you give up. If you've given up, it is time to give yourself new hope. If you've been unable to break a pattern, you can successfully do so now. Whether you take many small steps or one giant leap, if you're willing to keep moving forward, you will succeed.

Learn, Grow, Forgive evolved during my thirty years in private practice as a psychotherapist and addictions counselor. It was the tough cases, patients who lacked success in twelve-step programs and therapy, who challenged my professional skills. When patients would cry, "I can't get this," or "I'm stuck," I felt inadequate to help them. They were on a treadmill they abhorred, having lost faith in their ability to change or find refuge in a higher power, stuck in the depths of their deadly emotions. Robin Williams and Philip Seymour Hoffman were such unfortunates. If my patients were willing to do more in-depth work, I had to become a better therapist.

People who chronically relapse on alcohol, drugs, food, gambling, addictive relationships, sex, spending, or workaholism, or other self-sabotaging behaviors, think they cannot stop. They often give up hope of positive change and succumb to depression, destitution, and even suicide. You can change.

A situation becomes hopeless only when you stop trying. Of all the help offered for addictions, the twelve-step model is highly effective for abstinence, but it is not designed to heal the underlying trauma. There is only so much suffering a person can endure before giving up. It would be like investing countless hours studying for a critical test, just to fail again and again, or being unable to achieve goals or feel better after spending years in therapy or recovery meetings. Discouragement grinds away at every bit of hope, motivation, and success. Consumed with a sense of failure, the struggling person hears such clichés as "It works if you work it," "Live and let live," and "Keep coming back." While all of this is sound advice, it also fuels a sense of inadequacy in those who are struggling. When the goal seems unattainable, it is only natural to lose interest.

To further compound the problem, support systems—including therapists—often give up on patients perceived as "unwilling" or "doing it wrong." Helping someone who does not seem to improve can foster a sense of inadequacy and undermine the therapeutic alliance. Burnout is inevitable. As long as the patient is committed to the work, the helper must never give up. If a patient is not fully committed, there is nothing a healer can do.

I have found that healing is a two-way street for the patient and the therapist. A wounded healer can take a person only so far. I had to overcome my own blocks before I could help others break the barriers they were facing. Children can only be as well as their healthiest parent. The same applies to the therapeutic relationship. A therapist must have enough skill and emotional stability to take the patient through the barriers that inevitably surface in therapy, just as they do in the patient's closest relationships.

You must remember that you are making progress, even if it appears that you are not. Mental health progress is similar to getting in physical shape. You may go to the gym for a long time before you can see the results, but those changes have been happening since your very first workout. As you go through this process, you must remember that you never give up. The accumulation of subtle changes equals success.

The three-step process in this book will help those of you who feel trapped in negative patterns. You will learn how your psychological makeup has led to compulsive behaviors by understanding how the templates were formed and stored in your unconscious. Rather than succumbing to shame, you now perceive mistakes as learning tools. Instead of running from those unwanted feelings that seem all-consuming, you sit with the discomfort, feel it and accept it, and then grow beyond the pain. By focusing on your growth, no matter how little or slow, you will be able to keep moving forward.

When you have uprooted your emotional damage and replaced it with self-love and forgiveness, you heal at the core of your being. You lose tolerance for unloving acts that harm your body and mind, and through love, you develop a new spiritual connection.

Deidra was a patient who learned how to look at herself and her life in a new way. When she first started therapy, she would act out sexually whenever she felt depressed, which only made her more depressed. She compared it to her old days of a hangover after drinking and then drinking too much again. Now two years sober, she realized she was merely substituting sex for alcohol. Deidra had therapy, attended a sex addiction program, and read several books on love addiction, but her low self-esteem intensified when she could not break her pattern. When she committed to the learn, grow, and forgive process, there were many times when she would be angry with me when I asked her to be with her feelings rather than medicate them with sex. Eventually, she was able to recognize I was not a controlling mother figure, and she was able to replace that image with someone who was there to support her growth.

As trust in the therapy grew, Deidra stopped judging herself when she fell short of her goals and was able to explore the feelings she had avoided. As her pain surfaced and she mourned, Deidra began to gain confidence in her ability to cope without acting out. The more she focused on herself, the more she transformed into a woman with dignity and self-respect. After a year of therapy, Deidra had learned the source of her lifelong suffering, and she was willing to grow by working through her pain and then was able to forgive herself and others.

If you spent a great deal of time in therapy, read self-help books, and are still seeking answers, do not give up. You might be in a self-perpetuating cycle, or maybe you lost hope and stopped trying to get better. When you learn how you got in the maze, you can also learn how to get out. You must allow for mistakes as valuable learning experiences. No matter how many times you have to keep trying, never give up on yourself. Once the patterns change, so will your life. The important thing is that you do not give up, no matter what. You are worth the effort.

This three-step process will describe in detail how you can take any situation in your life and move it from the failure column to the success column. If you are relentless, this process will work for you. Your entire life will begin to make sense in a way that you had not previously considered. All the misfortunes of your past will transform into gratitude, giving you richer, more profound experiences. What could be more important than compiling the pieces of your life to form a tapestry that is a perfect work of personal art and history? There may be a couple of stitches out of place, but they, too, add to your unique life story.

My greatest hope is that you will use the three-step process outlined in *Learn, Grow, Forgive* to see that success is within your grasp. In time, as you gain mastery over the internal conflicts and move beyond them, you will witness how your outer life reflects those changes in ways that you never thought possible.

The case histories presented here have been modified to protect the confidentiality of these patients.

Part I

Learn

1

Chapter

The Origins of Self-Destruction

I have not failed; I've just found ten thousand ways that won't work.
—Thomas Edison

Long before you developed a self-destructive pattern, a feeling of discontent was forming within you. To *learn* means having the courage to face your past, face the effect it had on you, and determine if you've avoided that discomfort by using people, places, and things to medicate those feelings. If you are willing to change, you can; you need only know how.

From the moment of birth, our concepts of ourselves and other people begin to form. From then on, what we are taught, or not taught, is how we become set in our ways—good or bad. Babies are innocent and free from societal programming. When nurtured and taught love and respect for themselves and others, they become well-adjusted and happy. When parents teach children to share and receive love, they will naturally integrate the needs of self and others (rarely the case in the dysfunctional family).

Child-rearing errors pass on from generation to generation, many based on fear rather than love. Our caretakers did not necessarily intend to harm us. Adults are not handed a manual on marriage or the perfect way to raise a child. Until recently, there was little information available on the best child-rearing practices. Even worse, children raised in families that were suffering from addictions, mental health problems, and other dysfunctions were at the mercy of people who were too ill to know what they were doing. Children brought up in these environments often find themselves following in the footsteps of the very people they vowed never to emulate. Many of these young people grow maladjusted and wind up in therapy, diagnosed with all types of psychiatric disorders. These labels often miss the mark and ignore the underlying trauma that precipitated the diagnosis.

In Truth We Trust

Children have no problem seeing the truth, but when young people are told they cannot trust what they see, hear, and feel, they must choose between illusion or reality. Children's survival depends on trusting the ones on whom their lives depend. When parents disavow their child's perception, distrust of one's intuition is replaced with the other's lie. There is a cost for this repudiation; those same broken, unresolved schisms are reenacted throughout one's life.

You may have been deluded when you were young, but you do not have to live a lie now. If you want to heal, you have to be willing to embrace the truth.

Resistance Prevention: Identify the Blocks

If you've been in a pattern you cannot break, you will need to clear yourself of any blocks that may have prevented your success. The first block to overcome is resistance. Many of us grew up in constrictive environments or homes with impossible rules. If a child is raised with too many rules, rules that do not make sense, or rules that have a double standard, these things can cause a young mind to shut down or rebel. Before you can learn how to heal, you must reprogram your thinking with open-mindedness and truth.

When Sharon first came into my office, she was emotionally detached and not sure what brought her to therapy. She told me her parents never allowed her to decide for herself, and they said that only "weak people went to shrinks." She said the only reason she made an appointment was that her daughter insisted. Sharon went from doing what her parents wanted to what her daughter wanted, without having any internal sense of need for herself. Careful that we avoid the same trap, at the end of the session, I suggested that she give some time and thought to why she had spent her life doing what others wanted. I also suggested she wait to start therapy until *she* was ready, not when others thought it was time.

Three years later, Sharon made a second appointment. By then, her husband had divorced her because he was "sick of living with the Ice Queen." Sharon was shocked, but it was the jolt she needed to resuscitate her life. She was now ready to do the work that would help her to heal and recapture her forgotten self.

Rebellion is another reactive block that you must overcome if you want to have freedom from bondage. To be against something only because you were raised to act or believe a certain way is closed-minded and prevents learning. If you rebel against a belief system you were forced to endure, you are still a victim of that belief system. If you refuse to explore your own thoughts and feelings, you are living a robotic life.

One patient, Arthur, wanted to be more spiritual, but he hated going to church because it did not make sense to him that "God was supposed to be loving but also wrathful." He told me, "I do not like being controlled by some invisible old man in the sky." By the time he left home, he had vowed he would never set foot in a church again. Arthur was rightly rejecting something that did not make sense, but he also rejected something that he had never given any personal thought. Now is the time to think for yourself.

Substituting one addiction for a different one is another blockage that prevents learning and change. Addictions are false substitutes for a genuine spiritual connection—feeling love. Stopping one addiction, such as alcohol, drugs, food, gambling, sex, overspending, sugar, work, and other deadly habits, without healing the taproot of the problem will only lead to another form of self-medication. This merry-go-round will not allow you to get to the toxic root of your unhealed wounds. When I tried to quit smoking for the umpteenth time, one of the healers I sought help from asked me why it was so hard for me to stop.

I replied, "Because I love cigarettes; they have been my best friend ever since I was twelve years old."

She then replied, "When you can say you love yourself as much as you love cigarettes, you won't want to poison yourself anymore."

Once that thought took hold, I was free. As long as you try to get high through an addiction, you will never find your real higher power.

When we relate to people, places, and things as mere objects to fill an empty hole or numb pain, we remain in a maze. As *A Course in Miracles* says, we "search but never find." Well-adjusted people do not wander about with an umbilical cord, seeking to fill up with their next fix. They simply experience the joy of sharing and receiving what life has to offer. You must stop medicating your feelings if you want to change.

When I first met with Jeffrey, he told me when he went to AA and stopped drinking; he felt good about himself. His marriage improved, and stable income eliminated debt and provided financial security. Even though he was abstinent from alcohol, he became a nonstop coffee drinker and increased his cigarette smoking. At two years sober, under the pressure of his physician, he stopped these habits. Over the next year, Jeffrey gained so much weight that he could not fit into his clothes. He shamefully admitted he had been consuming a container of ice cream every night. Jeffrey came to therapy because he knew that the carton of ice cream was only creating a greater sense of lack. In treatment, Jeffrey learned that he was covering up emotions that he had carried all of his life. He had been sexually abused by an uncle when he was five years old. At family gatherings, his uncle would corner him and make sexual overtures toward him, once pinning Jeffrey against a wall, pressing against him, and reaching inside his pants. Jeffrey learned to stay clear of his uncle, but his innocence shattered with betrayal and shock was buried deep inside. In therapy, as he faced those memories and grieved the pain, he began to feel more comfortable in his own skin and more emotionally open to his family and life all around him.

Jeffrey was experiencing what many addicted people face: bouncing from one vice to the next, never discovering the deeper issues underneath the addiction. True freedom can only emerge from learning how to heal the emotions that are being medicated and replacing that void and pain with genuine love. Now is the time to get off autopilot and take control of your command center.

Feel It to Heal It

Many mental health professionals have adopted quick-fix methods to alleviate symptoms. While all types of therapy are helpful, some miss the core issues. Psychotropic medications are now the norm rather than the exception, and this form of treatment is often a substitute for psychological healing. Some drugs have a long-term effect on the chemistry of children's brains, treating the symptoms and masking the pain. However, people suffering from major depression, bipolar disorder, psychosis, and schizophrenia will need medicine before they can fully heal. These conditions do require certain drugs, just as a person with diabetes needs insulin. Once stabilized, these individuals can then do more in-depth work to heal the underlying pain not associated with the chemical imbalance.

Some cognitive therapies only bypass an unhealed past by covering it up with better thoughts. No doubt, logical, rational thinking is preferable to self-destructive thoughts, but sometimes, like medication, those therapies can ignore the underlying causes of the depression, mask the pain, and ignore the need for emotional healing.

Another progress-blocker occurs under the false notion that religion or spirituality cures all problems. Frequently, people think that if they are angry or upset, or they dig up the past, they are not spiritual. Using any cliché—religious or otherwise—is just another way of avoiding how you truly feel. This form of diversion does not get to the core problem. We must embrace our feelings and work through the associated pain before we can experience a spirituality that nourishes us.

If you want to heal, you must persevere and keep your commitment to yourself by staying in the therapeutic process. You must be willing to go back to the place where you first started to escape your feelings and learn new ways to heal those emotions so that you can achieve the life you want. If you've spent your whole life avoiding your innermost thoughts and feelings, you cannot expect this process to be fast or easy. To break through your walls, you need to remain engaged until you are restored to happiness. Once you are free from the past, your tolerance for pain will be gone. Chaos will no longer be compatible with your healed state of mind, and serenity will be your foremost priority. Be patient with yourself, keep doing the work, and trust that you will achieve your goals. You will succeed.

Love All of You, Perfectly Flawed

Dr. Elizabeth Kubler-Ross, an expert on the emotional process of death and dying, tells us life is full of lessons that are meant for us to learn, and we are not supposed to be perfect. One of my patients brought her dog to therapy. When I asked her if she thought her dog was perfect, she told me, "Of course not. I wouldn't love him nearly as much if he didn't have that crooked ear and two different-colored eyes." When you can love your human flaws, you will be able to enjoy loving yourself and others.

It's Never Too Late to Have a Happy Adulthood

Some of us have been taught to learn from our mistakes, but not everyone can do so. When you learn why you make those mistakes in the first place, you will no longer be a victim; you are taking the first step to self-love. You may have been forced to do things when you were young, but now you are free to make your own choices. Regardless of the circumstances, no one has control over your mind without your consent.

I once had a birthday party for a friend, and when I asked him what he wanted for his birthday, he said a blue birthday cake. When he was little, his best friend had a blue cake, but his mother only let him have vanilla. As a surprise, I made a blue ice cream cake decorated with blue frosting and blue candles. I will never forget my friend's little-boy eyes reflecting the sixty lighted candles when he saw his everything-blue birthday cake.

At any point in time, you can give yourself what you did not receive when you were young: the ultimate freedom from victimhood. You can never go back in time, but you always have now. Now is the time to give yourself the parenting you didn't receive when you were a child.

In the following pages, you will learn about imprints and templates and how they formed in your unconscious. Short exercises at the end of each chapter will help you to recognize how your childhood programming is currently manifesting itself in your life. This work is designed to free you from blaming yourself or others and teach you how to replace those reactions with empowering tools for psychological and spiritual healing. You will be able to record your answers and insights in journal form so that you can identify the patterns that have dominated your life. Once this awareness takes place, you have the power to change.

Moment of Reflection: What Was It Like?

1. Describe how your parents interacted with each other when you were young.

2. What early memories stand out in your family life?

3. What things were painful and made you feel confused?

4. How did you cope with those painful feelings?

5.a. In what ways were you taught about how to act, feel, and think? List the rules that you had to follow.

____

____

____

5.b. Which rules did not make sense to you?

____

____

____

6.a. If you were the parent, what guidelines would you have instead of those that were imposed on you? How would you do things differently?

____

____

____

6.b. Are you willing to follow those self-designed guidelines now? ____________________

7. Were you indoctrinated in a way that you did not like? If so, describe what you were taught. Are you willing to explore spirituality from a different perspective?

____

____

____

8. What did you do to cope with emotional pain? How do you cope now?

____

____

____

9. Are you willing to learn new ways to feel and to express your emotions? If you were comfortable with your feelings and how to express them, what would that look like? How might you resist that process? Close-minded, transfer addictions, conforming, rebelling?

____

Additional Journal Space

2

Chapter

Understanding the Template

You see only the past. It is the reason why you are never upset for the reason that you think.
A Course in Miracles

Each of us has a template that formed from our childhood experiences. If you drew a picture of your family and put a frame around it, that would be your template for life. It is an image forever ingrained in your mind, and it can represent pleasure, pain, or anywhere in between. Without your realization, it governs you and rules your decisions. When you veer off the path, you will feel lost, even when you are not.

Our template causes us to gravitate to people and relationships like our family of origin. Pleasant or unpleasant, there is a familiarity in being with people who remind us of those significant others from our youth. That is what drives a child of an alcoholic to marry an alcoholic or addict (or become one). Before you can change these templates, first you must learn how they formed and how you are currently reenacting them.

Sandy was able to see how her past was controlling her and how she worked through her fear. Growing up under her mother's constant disapproval—getting critical looks or negative comments—took a long-term toll on her. She said this behavior was so persistent; it made her think her mother didn't like her. This feeling of being unaccepted was unbearable, and Sandy slowly disconnected from her feelings. She always wondered what was wrong with her and kept trying to seek her mom's approval. "I thought if I had the right friends, then she would like me," she said, "but instead, she criticized them. When I went away to college, I went home as little as possible, and this helped, but the damage to my self-esteem had already happened. I was married twice, both for three years, twenty-eight years apart. The men in those marriages and the few other men with whom I was involved shared a similar trait: They were all self-absorbed. I interpreted this as a sign I should try harder so that they, too, would like me. They didn't."

Sandy realized this theme carried forward her entire life. Kind men who seemed to like her were of no interest to her; their personalities were not familiar enough. She gravitated toward people who did not show much warmth or affection, and she felt "stuck" in the pattern of trying harder, operating under the clear message that she had to be the one to make a relationship work. Much later in life, Sandy moved closer to help her mother, thinking time and maturity would help, but to no avail. There was always friction, and she never felt the affection she craved from her mom. When she started to learn, grow, and forgive, she realized her blocked feelings from those earlier experiences had solidified this pattern in all of her relationships. After she worked through her feelings and realized the lack of affirmation was not her fault; she felt a sense of peace.

Now that her pattern is clear, she is aware of how her unconscious pulls her to people who are critical and negative, but she no longer is controlled by that unseen force. She told me, "I can now make better decisions by staying connected to my feelings, trusting them without running away, and choose to be with loving and warm people who clearly do like me."

If you are to step into the life that you want, you must believe that you can, be willing to do the work, and keep doing it until you succeed.

How the Template Forms

You were born to be happy. If you became dysfunctional, something happened to make you that way. Even children with major disabilities can have fulfilling lives when they are properly nurtured.

Our first relationships start at birth and form our psychological templates, the foundations for all lifelong bonding. When caretakers are not safe and loving, every aspect of our life is affected. Trauma and poor maternal bonding can lead to a pain template.

As early as 1924, Sigmund Freud, the founder of psychoanalysis, developed his theory on the significance of the attachment between a mother and her child. Freud postulated that ideally, a mother would hold her infant close while breastfeeding and emanate love to the infant through eye-to-eye contact, approving smiles, and gentle caresses. From that point forward, both positive and negative experiences become mentally etched in the infant's mind. When there is enough food, shelter, love, and touching, the child is content, resulting in the formation of a positive bond. When these basic needs are not satisfied, there is a permanent sense of scarcity of comfort, food, and love, creating an endless search for satisfaction. When we heal from this fear-based sense of lack, we can satisfy our needs in healthy ways.

Hold Me Close; Let Me Go

Throughout early development, the more a child's mother is attuned to her child, the better the connection. The best bonding occurs when there is a balance of closeness and separation. Too much or too little creates a faulty attachment and can later lead to intimacy conflicts. Feeding instead of soothing, holding too long or too tight, and micromanaging a child are the behaviors of a parent who is taking care of her own needs rather than making a conscious effort to do what is best for her child.

When the mother is distant or emotionally unavailable, the unfulfilled need for closeness creates a painful bond, a feeling of emptiness. Mothers who are distracted—like reading a magazine or staring into space—are not noticing their baby in their arms. In these cases, we find people who might be highly successful in specific areas of their lives but who are unable to form loving human attachments.

When Jay came to see me, he told me his nanny raised him. He wanted to spend time with his parents, but they were always traveling. When they were around, rather than chatting, cuddling, playing games, or going to the movies, his parents lectured him about his future and the importance of success. He received the most attention when he made good grades and showed an interest in following in their footsteps: attending boarding schools and Ivy League colleges. When he was forty-five, wealthy, but divorced (because he "did not know how to listen, be affectionate, or make love"), he realized that there were "huge flaws" in his character. Jay wanted more out of life than a massive financial portfolio, and in therapy, he learned how to connect to the neglected boyhood parts of himself. As his feelings became an integrated part of his personality, he learned how to be emotionally available. By the time he completed treatment, he was engaged to a woman with whom he shared a genuine bond.

As a baby grows into a toddler, it is a time of breaking away and becoming independent while still being the center of attention. The mother who smothers her child with overinvolvement creates a pain template. Too much attention or control causes a desire to move away from—rather than toward—the caregiver.

Mariah told me the predominant feeling she had growing up was that she could not wait to get away from her mother. She was never out of her mother's sight and not allowed to decide what to wear, what to eat, or with whom to play. Her mother "hovered over" her, causing her to feel suffocated. When she tried to pull away, her mother would not speak to her, which made her feel guilty. She fluctuated between feeling resentful and being ashamed for having such "hateful" feelings toward her very own mother. She counted the days when she could leave home, but even after going away to college, she felt like her mother was stalking her. She avoided getting close to people because she feared they would smother her or would want something from her; she did not want to give. She spent most of her college years in painful isolation.

Mariah recognized that she had formed a pain template with an overly involved parent, who made her feel either smothered or abandoned; ultimately, it led her to isolation. Therapy was particularly hard for her because it triggered old feelings of being controlled and forced to do things she did not want to do. Mariah wanted help, but part of her was sabotaging the support offered. She would "forget" appointments, be "too busy," or say she had to stop therapy because of money. Eventually, by freely expressing her frustration with the commitment of weekly visits, she was able to see that her resistance to therapy was related to the past—her fear of being micro-managed by her mother. Once she made this connection, she was internally motivated.

The paternal template with children is also an essential part of building positive relationships. When a father balances love and affection with appropriate discipline, he develops a healthy bond with his children.

Daddy's Little Princess Becomes Husband's Beloved Queen

When a man's daughter feels that she is unconditionally loved and adored, and he teaches her she is to be treated with respect, she will value herself with men in the future. Georgia, even though in recovery for alcoholism, had a very healthy sense of herself as a woman. Her father adored her. Georgia had many loving memories of her father doting on her, and she knew she was "the apple of his eye." At the same time, he would not allow her to disrespect him or herself. He taught her that a man was not worthy of her attention unless there was mutual respect. For example, on dates, the young man had to meet her father and assure him that he would be taking good care of his daughter, and she was not to get into his car unless he opened the door for her. Though she hated it at the time, Georgia's dad gave her a positive template of self-respect. That is why at two years sober, Georgia met the man of her dreams, became engaged, and married someone who adored her.

When closeness between a father and his daughter is missing, daughters will look for that validation elsewhere, settling for less than they deserve. A woman will alienate a man when she demands respect that she does not have for herself. She will get the love she wants only by forming a new positive template through healing the loss with her father and learning how to respect herself. If your father was not a good role model, you could find a surrogate through therapy or a trusted elder. A paternal bond combined with a spiritual connection to a loving source will provide all you need to honor yourself as a person to be treasured.

I Am My Father's Son

Ideally, a dad mentors his son, teaches him life skills and builds his confidence through supporting his independence and success. This positive template encourages a young man to grow into the man he wants to be. When a father berates his son and tells him he is worthless or he will never amount to anything, he shatters his son's self-confidence and cripples his self-esteem. This pain template programs a son to fulfill his father's unconscious curse upon him. He will not understand why he does not succeed and how this programming prevents him from his own success.

When a father sees his son as a rival rather than his child, this also creates a template for pain. This father is unconsciously jealous of his son's youth and abilities. He will be overly competitive with him in sports, flirt with his son's dates, and otherwise undermine his son's manliness. To avoid the possibility of feeling inferior, some fathers keep their son financially dependent. He conveys a hidden message that his son should never do better than he, lest he betray his father.

Picard, a thirty-year-old underachiever, told me that when he became a teenager, his father started treating him like a rival. His father often spoke of his own successes, forever informing Picard that he had "big shoes to fill." He would compare his looks to Picard, telling him that he was not as tall or muscular. He would insist on playing tennis until Picard would give up and let his dad win, and he constantly reminded Picard that he had several girlfriends by the time he was Picard's age. Picard felt both angry and embarrassed that his father put him in a competitive role and guilty when he outperformed his father. Without any resolution, these roles are intermittently played without either person stopping the game. Picard's journey to success began once he identified his unconscious guilt and permitted himself to reach his own potential regardless of anyone's conflicts.

The Twisted Bond of Trauma

In addition to bonding, unresolved trauma also plays a significant role in a child's emotional development. Some parents begin a family with their unhealed trauma. When this happens, there can be a lack of emotional stability, and children in these families often suffer abuse. When child abuse is severe, and the internal distress exceeds a reasonable level of tolerance, then a pain template is formed.

Abuse can be emotional, physical, sexual, or neglect—and either covert or overt. Children love their parents, no matter what.

When the people they love abuse them, they get a twisted view of relationships and often confuse love with pain.

There is plenty of room for error in any family, but too much distress overwhelms a child. There are rare cases when children are exceptionally wise and independently seek help outside of the home. I have heard stories of a friend, relative, or teacher who gently guided a troubled youngster toward a successful path. In the absence of a mentor, children raised by parents who are addicted, overly dependent, or unable to care for their family, or whose lives are unmanageable, will carry the trauma forward, forcing their children to endure emotions that they are not equipped to manage. This type of upbringing forms a pain template.

Mixed Messages Mess Us Up

Parents who say one thing and do the opposite cause confusion in their children. Marvin sought therapy to learn why he could not commit. He told me his dad worked hard in construction but drank a lot, so the family did not have much extra money. He often wondered why his parents had five children when they could barely make ends meet. They were Catholic and had to follow the sacraments, even when they didn't make sense. Marvin felt his parents loved each other, and the family was close, but he also felt confused. He wanted to be on the soccer team, but his parents could not afford the uniforms, yet they were always donating money and time to the church. Marvin got a job at age fourteen, but all of that income went to his parents to help pay the bills. He remembered feeling resentful that there was always money for beer and church but not for the things the family needed. His template represented family as being strapped down and never having enough, and he blamed "their God" for that.

Even though Marvin perceived his childhood as loving, the financial limitations due to spending on alcohol and religion created mixed messages that formed a pain template in his mind. As an adult,

Marvin was unable to commit because he intertwined marriage and religion as a place of deprivation, sacrifice, and struggle, rather than feeling a sense of abundance and cohesion. Once Marvin understood the role that alcohol—covered up with religion—played in his family, he was able to understand the root cause of his feeling of financial lack. When he recognized the backwardness of his family dysfunction, he was able to replace those values with his own standards for money and spirituality.

It's Just Too Painful Here

Children who are berated, manipulated, screamed at, or prematurely placed in an adult role are suffering from abuse. For example, parents exploit children when they use them as confidants or advisers. Children do not have the life experiences to counsel their parents, and they should not be put in the middle. One patient, Jessie, recognized her pattern of being attracted to women in bad relationships who needed excessive emotional support. Soon after meeting someone, she found herself in the role of "resident therapist." As a young teen, her parents came to her for advice about their relationship. She resented being the adult and having to hear what was wrong with a parent. Even though Jessica's parents did not intend to abuse her emotionally, their actions caused her to feel responsible for their happiness, placing her as the third person in their marriage. This type of triangulation keeps everyone stuck in what psychologist Eric Berne calls the victim, rescuer, persecutor role—a triangular merry-go-round of dysfunction. One parent (victim) runs to the child (rescuer) for help from the other parent (persecutor). Often when the child defends the parent, that same parent will criticize the child for interfering. Without any resolution, these roles are intermittently interplayed. Healthy parents work out their conflicts with each other, and they protect their children from being placed in surrogate roles.

I Trust—That I Cannot Trust

Broken promises, belittling, and invalidation are other forms of emotional abuse. Children feel secure when their parents follow through with commitments and provide a safe place to express feelings. When parents are unreliable and punish a child for saying so, these children learn to distrust.

Sam recognized that he was unable to trust anyone. He recalled numerous times when his parents promised him an allowance, gifts, or outings, but they rarely followed through. He suffered letdowns after being dismissed by his parents, who said they never made the promise in the first place. "When I cried, they told me I was ungrateful, and that if I did not straighten up, they would give me something to cry about." He remembered having deep bouts of depression, isolation, and he rarely looked forward to anything. In therapy, Sam resolved his pain template by learning to choose people he could count on and stayed away from those who did not keep their word. Most important, he learned it was his parents who were at fault, not his own innocent expectations.

Where, Oh Where, Did My Innocence Go?

Sexual abuse leaves a profound and lasting sense of shame on its survivors. I have seen many male and female patients who have connected their eating disorders to this problem. They either wanted to get so thin they would disappear or so heavy they would feel hidden; in either case, they attempted to feel protected from the perpetrator. Other patients, plagued by the unconscious reenactment of those early experiences, continue to be exploited or become perpetrators, reenacting the same horrors that happened to them. Some parents know that their children are sexually abused, but they do nothing to stop the crime. This type of child-sacrifice creates mental pain and anguish of the highest degree.

Sexual abuse might be either covert or overt. Covert sexual abuse occurs when a parent uses a child as a substitute partner. Thomas sought therapy because he wanted to break free from his mother, whom he felt treated him like her husband most of his life. "My parents lived in completely separate worlds. My mother told her secrets to me, asked me what she should wear, and made me accompany her to adult social events." Thomas had a pattern of being attracted to women who pursued him but were married to someone else. His treatment centered on grieving the loss of his childhood innocence and learning the healthy roles between a man and a woman.

A sexually overt parent makes physical or verbal advances (either consciously or unconsciously) in such a way that treats the child as a sexual object rather than a vulnerable young person to be protected at all times. Only deeply disturbed individuals use children for sexual gratification. Healthy adults choose confidants and intimate partners who are other grown-ups, not children they are supposed to be parenting.

Sticks and Stones Will Break My Bones, but Words Will Break My Spirit

Speaking to a child in an unloving or cruel manner may not seem abusive, but it's just as likely to leave a definitive mark on the child's self-image. Children can understand punishment for a specific wrongful act, but words that cut too deep can break their spirit. Almost every male alcoholic I ever worked with had a father who repeatedly berated him. When Baxter's father was angry, he would say he was a loser and would never amount to anything. His father programmed him for a self-fulfilled prophecy, and Baxter repeatedly sabotaged his own financial success. He worked diligently to learn why he felt useless and mourned the pain that those messages had instilled in him. He was then able to break his self-defeating patterns.

Children who don't feel welcomed in a family will suffer a sense of inferiority. Mary Beth started therapy when she realized her childhood was riddled with abuse and lack of care. Her mother frequently told her that she was not a planned pregnancy, "a mistake." Her father was "a tall, dark-haired, blue-eyed handsome man." Mary Beth felt like "a puppy dog waiting by the living-room bay window for his car to pull in the driveway at night." He would walk in the door, never look at her, walk right into the kitchen, and fix a drink. When she would try to hug him, he would say, "Not now, can't you see I'm exhausted? Children should be seen and not heard." As the years passed, the emptiness grew, and so did the pain from wishing and wondering why her parents did not show her love. By the time she was a teenager, she had tried to make up for that lack by getting attention from boys who only wanted sex. The more she tried to fill her void with men who did not love her, the more her emptiness grew. In therapy, Mary Beth was able to see how she was repeating the same pattern she had with her parents. Healing meant she would need to recognize intimacy was her parents' lack—not hers. Mary Beth was willing to face her past and do the work in therapy to heal her pain template brought on by neglect. With courage and commitment to learn, grow, and forgive, she developed a new template. She learned how to validate herself, and she learned to receive care from herself and others. She learned what it meant to be seen and heard. She was then able to transfer this experience to more intimate relationships, including a fulfilling marriage and two children she parented well.

The core conflict in all of these situations is that trust—the building block of all future relationships—has been corroded and corrupted. Recovery is about examining your painful family-relations model and replacing it with a healthier one. You can successfully achieve this through therapy because the therapist becomes a surrogate parent. If you seek treatment, it is essential that you find a healthy, skilled therapist. Safe boundaries of reliability, emotional support, respect, and loving conflict resolution create a new model for relationships.

I Can Rebuild a Better Me

The significance of the pain template is that it tends to reenact itself throughout your life. It places you under a hypnotic spell driven by your unconscious, and paradoxically, is trying to heal the past by changing it in the now. This will not work, but you can change your current behavior by healing your past. Most recovery programs tell us "doing the same thing over and over again and expecting different results" is the definition of insanity. As mentioned in the prologue, you can change this slogan to "Sanity is doing the same thing over and over again and getting different results." You get different results when you work through your pain rather than veering away from the discomfort.

To stop a particular behavior that does not serve you, you will need to recognize that your current reactions are embedded deeply in your unconscious, the areas in need of healing before you can break your pattern. If something upsets you, and you quickly brush it off, then you are not stuck in the emotions of prior experiences. However, if something causes a reaction in you, and your mind stays on nonstop rewind, then you can be sure it has a root deep within your unconscious. These are the feelings that propel you in the wrong direction time and time again.

A *Course in Miracles* teaches, "I see only the past," to remind us of this very fact. Most reactions to life are just the tip of the iceberg. There is a piece of the past, an old wound that lies hidden within the heart and mind. Whenever a new similar event bumps into that old tender spot, we react to that first unhealed wound. This is comparable to someone accidentally stepping on your toe, and it feels like that person has stomped on a broken toe that throbs for hours, rather than a minor "ouch" that quickly subsides. For example, the childhood pain of being rejected by someone you love could be reactivated by the slightest perceived rejection because it triggers old pain. Something as simple as a friend who cancels lunch could cause you to think of yourself (or the other person) as being unlikeable.

The same is true for pleasant experiences. Good memories now are the result of similar past experiences. If going out for ice cream was a pleasant childhood experience, you relive a happy memory every time you eat ice cream.

While there is no such thing as a perfect family, a sense of security is required for a youngster to form an image that the world is an abundant and comfortable place. Parents who are affectionate, talk to their children, have mutual respect, and teach healthy independence have conveyed stability even when faced with financial struggles or emotional hardships. When the emotionally bonded family experiences a traumatic event, they are unified to heal their pain. They share the challenge, and thus they recover from life's traumas. Children who grow up in this environment develop a pleasure template regarding life.

Even if you do not remember your childhood, you can draw inferences from the way you reenact those early experiences. The emotional DNA that is passed down from one generation to the next is evident by looking at the family tree. A person raised in a home with substance abuse is likely to become a substance abuser or marry one. Someone who had an unfaithful parent tends to cheat on their spouse or marry someone who cannot be faithful. A child who is comforted with food instead of emotional support is likely to have an eating disorder. If there was not enough physical nurturing, there is a tendency to gravitate toward sex addiction or avoid intimacy altogether. Remember, you were not born dysfunctional, and if you are currently engaging in self-destructive behavior, something happened to cause this.

When your desire to gain new knowledge overrides the pull to stay in darkness, you will be able to change your perception from hopeless to hopeful.

I thought I would never break my pattern of attracting unfaithful men. One of my therapists had told me that good-looking, successful men were the kind of men who were attracted to many women and vice versa. This message made me think that if I dated men who were less attractive and less successful, I could protect myself. That didn't work. Then I thought by being vulnerable and sharing my previous betrayals, no one would inflict more pain upon me. This too failed. With the learn, grow, and forgive process, I realized the insanity of trying to control things outside of myself. When I started to use a painful situation as a vessel to an old wound, I healed the past and grew.

My biggest leap happened when I decided I was not going to focus on this issue any further. My mind was no longer available to rent space to something for which I had no control. There was no use denying that I liked good-looking, ambitious men. Rather than trying to control my reactions, when my insecurities arose, I kept learning and growing each time I reacted. One day, when I was worrying about whether or not I could trust someone, a clear message came through: "You can trust yourself, and that is the only person you ever need to trust." I began to believe that I would be all right, no matter what the outcome. I was now free to replace a sense of insanity and failure with a new sense of sanity and faith. This has worked out.

To learn is to understand what went wrong and how it has affected you. Once you identify these templates, you can target the specific areas that need to heal. If you use the tools to learn, grow, and forgive, you will be able to parent yourself.

When we heal, we keep the good memories, and we transform our old painful memories into compassion and understanding for ourselves and others. We are then free to fill our lives with as many good times as possible. Now is the time to build new, happy memories.

The following exercises will help you recall memories that formed your template about relationships and how you would like them restructured:

Moment of Reflection: Understanding Your Template

1. When you were growing up, did you feel secure? Was there enough affection, attention, food, housing, shelter, and time together as a family? If not, what was lacking?

2. Did you feel safe? How were you disciplined? What made you feel unsafe? What made you feel safe?

3. Did it feel like your parents were mature adults? Did you feel that you were a replacement partner for one of your parents? What happened that made you feel that way? How would you have wanted it to be?

4. Did your mother instill confidence in you? If so, how? If not, how?

5. Did your father instill confidence in you? If so, how? If not, how?

6. Did you feel like you had a good bond with your mother and father? Did you feel like your parents were physically and emotionally present for you? Did you feel abandoned or smothered? What does healthy bonding look like to you?

7. Identify some of the same patterns that you have copied from your childhood?

8. Describe your template (positive or painful). Do you have good memories or memories of emotional, physical, or verbal pain?

9. Describe what a healthy template looks like to you.

____

____

____

10. Describe the patterns that you want to break.

____

____

____

11. What will your life look like once you break these patterns?

Additional Journal Space

3

Chapter

The Psychology of Imprinting

Love looks not with the eyes but with the mind.
And therefore is winged Cupid painted blind.
—William Shakespeare, *Midsummer Night's Dream*

Do you remember the thrill of your first crush? Did your heart go pitter-patter along with your racing thoughts of that unforgettable face? Unlike the template formed on a series of childhood experiences, a romantic imprint is mentally branded from a single life event.

In 1935, zoologist Konrad Lorenz noticed that newly hatched ducklings would follow the first object they saw, even if it were not a duck. He concluded that the first imprint is all that registered in the memory of the newly hatched ducklings.

Our minds also imprint, particularly in love and romance. The first crush sets the imprint for all future encounters. The first physical attraction is so powerful; it creates a lifelong pursuit of that same initial rush. The unforgettable attraction stirs the senses each time a similar image presents itself—a mental imprint that overrides all else. If a young man imprints on a tall, dark-haired, blue-eyed girl, his preference will be mostly for girls with those characteristics. If a young girl imprints on a blond-haired, brown-eyed boy, she will gravitate toward these features throughout her life. Not because of the looks but, instead, the visceral response that particular memory stirs.

Sometimes, imprints and templates collide. You can be mesmerized by someone's looks, only later to find out that your personalities are complete opposites.

Deborah describes this perfectly: "I was head over heels the moment I saw Billy. His tousled brown hair and sparkling blue eyes reminded me of my first boyfriend. The only problem: We had completely different values. He was from an alcoholic family, and he drank excessively. My parents didn't drink, and I never touched the stuff."

She described Billy as footloose and fancy-free, and herself as super-responsible. The passion was great, but the fighting was pure misery. Deborah said the conflicts went on for so long that she felt like she was on autopilot, too worn out to take responsibility for the insanity. In the third session, she confessed, "I don't think that my feelings for Billy have anything to do with love. There is some unknown force inside me that is trying to make the impossible work. In all honesty, I don't really want to be with Billy."

While Deborah and Billy had a powerful imprint match, their templates were utterly incongruent. They were so far apart and unable to agree on much of anything, making it impossible for them to give to each other in ways that were appreciated or fulfilling. Most of their energy went into nonstop problem-solving rather than enjoying each other's company. Deborah's recovery began when she realized that crazy attraction did not equal love. She would have to learn the origins of her pain template and heal it if she were to have a satisfying relationship.

Create Your Own Script

A new duckling might imprint on the first object it sees, such as a turtle, but the two will never be compatible. People cannot rely on imprints to make smart romantic choices. When physical attributes override essential factors such as communication, similar interests, and shared values, the relationship will struggle.

From the time Tom and Kristina met, they were magnetically drawn to each other. They locked eyes in a bar, and for the entire evening, they were oblivious to everything else. After a few drinks, they left the bar and went to Tom's place for wild, passionate sex. They were inseparable for the next few months, but once they started to know each other, they realized they had little in common. They began to bicker, which only tended to intensify the passion and sex when they were making up. Their incessant breakups took a toll on their positive feelings toward each other. When they came in for help, I asked about the basis of their attraction; they both admitted it was purely physical. By tracking the origins of those physical preferences, they came to understand that they were reenacting their childhood crushes. Kristina thought Tom looked like her handsome older cousin, and Tom saw his fifth-grade crush in Kristina. Both were reenacting the imprints of being passionately stirred, blotting out all logic and reason. I recommended that Tom and Kristina restart their relationship, with really getting to know each other and finding areas of compatibility. Unfortunately, they were looking for a quick fix, and that was the last I saw of them.

Templates can collide with imprints in many ways. If a child is raised in a family with a working father and a stay-at-home mom and marries someone with a different template, the attraction imprint alone cannot sustain the relationship. If the partners grew up with different backgrounds, or if their cultural and religious beliefs conflict, these relationships often lack cohesion and sustainability.

Barbara came to see me after she was divorced. She and Harold were inseparable throughout their senior year of high school. Love at first sight, they rushed into a sexual relationship. When Harold went away to college, he did not adapt to campus life and was miserable without Barbara. After the first semester, he quit school to come home and marry Barbara—out of need more than love. Even though they both grew up in affluent homes, Barbara and Harold were raised quite differently. The women in Barbara's family were waited on by staff; the women in Harold's family waited on the family members. Barbara had never made a bed, done dishes, or turned on a vacuum cleaner. Upon getting married, she was unable to perform basic household tasks, even though that was her agreed-upon role. When Harold arrived home tired from work, he resented having to do the housekeeping and meal preparation. His frustration compounded when Barbara was disinclined to learn either skill, and she was hurt when he raised these issues with her. Things worsened after they had a child. Harold not only was the breadwinner and housekeeper but their daughter's primary caretaker as well. After just two short years, Harold filed for a divorce, leaving Barbara devastated and clueless.

In both of these cases, it is highly unlikely that either person will be able to adapt to the other unless they both recognize that common values will create more happiness than mere animal attraction. Being drawn to someone's looks might be exciting, but that alone will not override hard drives in the individual's template. It is important to note, however, that many people are drawn together because of their painful templates. If both people are committed to using their reactions to each other as opportunities to heal, they can enjoy a gratifying relationship that provides opportunities to learn and grow.

Energize the Possibilities, Not the Differences

Changing one's character is far more complicated than changing one's physical attributes. You can be attracted to someone who is not your perfect imprint and still fall in love. If you change your mind-set from perfection to appealing, you are more likely to find the kind of true love that is sustainable. The closer you feel to someone, the more attractive they become.

Bob told me that he usually dated tall redheads, even though none of those relationships lasted. He was willing to change his pattern of instant attraction for something more meaningful. He explored why he objectified women rather than focusing on how someone treated him. His role models had demonstrated that a woman's looks were much more important than her values. His father had married several times; each wife was beautiful but unable to give effort or time to the family. Bob witnessed marriage as the man providing financial security to women, whose only role was to look appealing. When these superficial benefits ran their course, there was not enough depth for the union to last.

Bob agreed to get to know someone before he decided to be emotionally or physically involved. When he met Candace, a petite blonde who was fun and caring, he decided to go slow. By giving her a chance, he discovered the assets that mattered most to him: talking, common interests, similar lifestyles, and backgrounds. As the relationship matured, he recognized that he felt more deeply about her than anyone prior, and more important, he felt a sense of trust he never experienced before. True love found its way to Bob's heart when he gave up his imprint as the sole criterion for his long-term happiness. When Bob learned about himself, he was able to move out of his old way of thinking and relate to a woman as an individual rather than rejecting someone who did not match his imprint.

Tango, Don't Tangle

In a healthy bond, both people enjoy being close and enjoy their time apart as well. This ebb and flow of closeness and distance provide fulfillment inside and outside of the relationship. Separate hobbies and interests keep a relationship vibrant. If someone feels smothered, boredom replaces desire. If there is not enough attention, the partner might seek attention elsewhere.

Relationships are not guaranteed to last forever. Sometimes, people are under the illusion that things have to be perfect or the union will fail. Fears from old templates can cause reactions that sabotage a sense of security. A fear-based relationship cannot thrive. Conflicts are a natural part of healthy relationships, making them real.

Mike and Jackie illustrate how differences can be resolved and replaced with intimacy. When they came in for couple's therapy, Mike told me that he noticed a pattern had emerged in his relationships with women. Initially drawn to attractive, bright women who offered long-term potential, Mike found himself bored within six months. After the third or fourth breakup, he decided to get help. As we explored the dynamics of his current relationship with Jackie, we were able to see what was happening. Mike's template was one of poor bonding with his mother. He did not receive much affection or attention from her, and it made him feel inferior. In early adulthood, he often found himself rejected by girlfriends, but as his financial success grew, he became the rejecter. He rushed into relationships that quickly fizzled. Now with Jackie, Mike could not understand why he wanted to break up with her when she was trying so hard to please him. He liked that Jackie was in college, worked hard, and was attractive, but he noticed he had become bored and was finding fault with her. It seemed the harder she tried, the worse things became.

It was clear that Mike and Jackie were both struggling with how to bond. For Mike, rejection was more familiar than closeness, but too much effort on Jackie's part was equally deadening of his desire. Mike did not know how to experience healthy intimacy—merging and distancing—with a woman. Bored with Jackie, he resorted to internet porn rather than having sex with her. Jackie would have to replace her mothering template with emotional self-sufficiency and learn to please herself more and Mike less. Mike would have to overcome boredom by being vulnerable and talking about his true feelings. As long as he kept attracting a woman who would do anything to keep him, rather than stand in her own truth while challenging him to grow, he would remain stuck in his indifference.

After three sessions, Jackie decided to stop therapy, stating, "I do not want to change; it's his problem, not mine." Mike continued his work, and ultimately, their relationship ended. By the time he completed treatment, he was able to date women who wanted to get to know him before rushing into a physical relationship. At first, it felt awkward, but as time went on, he liked forming an emotional attachment with someone before he had sex and found that an independent woman was more intriguing to him.

The Paradox of Attraction

Having differentiated physical attraction (imprint) and compatibility (template), we learned that most relationships are the reenactment of our early bonding (or lack thereof). Remember that our imprints and templates have programmed us to be attracted to those who resemble our childhood significant others. You can learn to be aware of this while you simultaneously learn to break unhealthy patterns. Impulsive attraction is one such pattern. Jumping prematurely into a relationship is like buying the first car or house you see, committing to a particular career without much forethought, or moving to a foreign country because someone told you they like it there. Learning about yourself and finding the best match for you may take some doing, but this effort pays off in the long run. You know what you like and what you don't like. If talking is important to you, find someone who enjoys a good conversation. If touch is vital, be with someone who is affectionate. If you crave alone time, search for someone who also values solace. If you enjoy a close bond, be with someone who is emotionally available. Balanced relationships have a combination of both deep intimacy and individuality.

No matter how perfect the imprint, no amount of physical attraction can withstand unrelenting conflict. You are the one who is responsible for knowing yourself and what traits are important to you. Do not settle for less.

The following exercises will help you identify your first romantic imprint as well as your family-of-origin values. You will be able to clarify the type of person you are most compatible with.

Moment of Reflection: Identifying Your Early Imprint

1.a. What are the similarities between that first crush (probably around the fifth grade) and those you are physically attracted to now? Describe that person in detail.

1.b. How have those early imprints served you? How have they limited you?

____

____

____

2. Do you take time to get to know a person, or do you jump into relationships too soon because of the attraction? If so, what pulls you in?

____

____

____

3. Have you ever been with someone who did not fit your imprint? Describe what this was like.

____

____

____

4. What were your mother's roles in the family?

5. What were your father's roles in the family?

6. If you put pure physical attraction aside, what values are the most important in a mate?

7. Who tries harder in your relationships? Do you allow space when it feels like someone is pulling back, or do you hold on tighter? Are you willing to be in the place of the unknown and wait for the right time to connect? Do you pull away and shut down? Are you willing to leave an opening for conversation and healing to take place?

8. Do you allow yourself to feel desire? How do you experience desire? Are you substituting another desire (an addiction) in place of love?

____

____

____

Circle the traits that best described you. Put a star by the most important.

Conversation

Physical intimacy: touch

Physical intimacy: sex

Good cook

Financially conservative

Same religion

Financially free, prefer to spend, not save

Similar backgrounds

Intelligence

Staying home

Neat and organized

Open personality

Time alone

Time with family

Time together

Introverted personality

Write your own

Additional Journal Space

4

Chapter

The Power of the Unconscious

A thing which has not been understood inevitably reappears; like an unlaid ghost, it cannot rest until the mystery has been resolved and the spell broken.
—Sigmund Freud

Your mind, just like your body, was designed to heal. When you are physically hurt, you acknowledge the pain, you tend to the injury, and then healing occurs. Your mind also can heal itself, but you must be willing to recognize the wound, tend to the injury, and allow the wound to mend. Recovery means you unleash repressed pain and allow yourself to face the past, grieve it, and learn how to love.

Sigmund Freud referred to the unconscious as the place where thoughts, feelings, memories, motivations, and all things unwanted are repressed in the mind, where they hide. When children are taught that certain impulses—particularly anger and sex—are unacceptable, they learn to reject these parts of themselves. If I feel hatred toward my mother, anger is wrong; it gets repressed. If I feel sexual, it is shameful; this, too, gets repressed.

Our repressed feelings and memories lurk beneath the surface of our conscious awareness, like a puppeteer waiting to pull our strings. It is these unresolved conflicts in our templates that we continually reenact. A part of us says, "I don't like what happened, and I want it to be different. This time, I will be able to master this situation." We are unknowingly trying to revise old traumatic events without the tools to create a different outcome. If you don't realize you are reenacting an old wound, you cannot correct the problem. Until you see that this obsessive part of you is trying to fix the past, you will remain powerless.

Explaining the psychoanalytic process in its entirety is beyond the scope of this book, but the main point is to recognize that uncomfortable memories and thoughts that the conscious mind wishes to avoid become lodged in the unconscious. Fortunately, that trap has a door.

Jim started therapy to break a pattern that was interfering with his happiness. His dad, a successful businessman and heavy drinker, was never home. As a youngster, Jim longed to spend time with him and cried every time his father left for another business trip. As Jim grew older, his sadness toward his father turned to hate and then to guilt for feeling such rage. By the time he was a teenager, Jim had used pot and alcohol to blot out all feelings toward his dad.

Jim's drinking was so bad by the time he turned thirty, he joined Alcoholics Anonymous. He did everything suggested, and he was able to stay sober. When he worked the recovery steps, he had no problem recognizing he was powerless over alcohol and that he needed a higher power. When he was told to look at his role in relationships, his repressed feelings of abandonment by his father surfaced. When his sponsor mentioned he "needed to just focus on himself and look at his own role," he only felt worse.

Jim said he honestly could not see any reason for his father's rejection; he was only a little boy who wanted to spend time with his dad. He wanted to do the program right, so he faked it and pretended that his anger was unjustified.

Jim was unconsciously reenacting his childhood pain in his adult life. He was unable to resolve the conflict as a wounded little boy who decided he would never be like his father. His insurance policy for this decision was never to have children of his own. He was attracted only to people who rejected him, and when they pulled away, he felt hurt and angry. His AA sponsor told him anger was a luxury he could not afford, which caused him to stuff his anger and feel trapped in internal turmoil.

Jim told me, "Something is seriously wrong with me. I feel like a total fake." He realized by suppressing emotions his entire life; he remained stuck in a pattern that blocked authentic love for himself and others.

Before Jim could fully heal, he had to face his pain template of an emotionally absent father. This conflict with the father Jim loved was being played out in his adult relationships. He kept his distance from most people, setting himself up to be unreasonably lonely. He allowed a few people in, but his ambivalence did not allow them to bond with him. Jim unknowingly replayed the same conflicts with his father that failed to provide the intimacy he craved yet feared. The little boy within Jim needed to voice his pain so that he could learn how to experience healthy closeness.

With more in-depth work, Jim was able to stop reenacting his unconscious template. Part of his therapy was to find a healthy male role model who could serve as a surrogate father. Even though he struggled with reliving his childhood anger and pain, he allowed a therapeutic relationship to guide him. He learned to feel the pain of emptiness and loneliness, work through the unresolved frustration with his father's indifference, and find solace in meditation, reading, golfing, and music. The more he sat with his feelings and found new interests, the more fulfilled he felt, and the more he was able to offer and receive in all of his relationships. Today, Jim has a cherished family—a wife and three children.

Mending the Broken Record

The repeated effort to heal an old wound by attempting to control the outcome is what Freud referred to as "repetition compulsion." The failed bonds with our caretakers are trying to repair themselves in ways that do not work. If your mother was full of rage, you might feel drawn to angry people you want to calm down. If your father was an alcoholic, you might be attracted to people with addictive personalities. Whatever longing you endured may still be haunting you and reappearing through your unconscious attractions. Rather than stay away from these people, you may be unconsciously drawn to fix them. A person must want help, and this must be a two-way street. Even more importantly, trying to fix an unwilling participant leaves you only broken and unhealed.

Identifying the original trauma is important, but that in itself will not stop your behavior. Your wound has to be faced and mourned, for as long as it takes, followed by the willingness to redirect all healing to only yourself. Otherwise, you will continue to do the same things over and over again and feel worse. The path out of the pain maze leads right through it.

Clear the Smoke from the Mirrors

Once you understand the compulsion to repeat the same mistakes, you can look at whatever you are trying to change in another person as the reflection of your own wound. If your focus is on someone else, you can learn to bring that message right back to yourself—but in a way that is healing. Are you trying to control someone's drinking because of an alcoholic parent? Are you trying to make an unsustainable relationship work because you watched your parents flounder? Do you manipulate someone into being with you because you felt abandoned or devalued as a child? Being caught in the illusion that we can fix someone, we miss the opportunity to heal ourselves. A *Course in Miracles* says we place ourselves in competition with God when we think we have the power to make someone see the light, we are assuming we know what is best for them. If we want to be emotionally and spiritually healthy, we must stop playing God, point our attention inward, and focus on the parts of ourselves that need help.

Doug, thirty years sober, struggled with a sexually inappropriate mother who caused him to be in deep confusion about healthy relationships. He told me he could not understand his relationships with women and could not commit to a long-term relationship. A Palm Beach playboy until age sixty, fear of dying alone propelled him to find a wife, but his choices had caused him to hit an emotional bottom. He was attracted to alcoholic women half his age who had children.

He told me, "I see them as helpless birds with broken wings"; whom he wanted to rescue. He recognized his compulsive pattern of helping emotionally broken women and caretaking their children, only to be drawn into emotional disaster again and again. In his last relationship, Doug found himself babysitting a five-year-old while his girlfriend was out barhopping all night long.

In spite of the pain, he described this relationship as "soulmates. It was the best sex I have ever experienced. Our relationship was either totally amazing or horrible." Doug was still reeling from the pain, even though it has been a year since the breakup. He was worried that he was going to drink again if he did not get help.

Doug's mother was beautiful, seductive, and alcoholic. An indelible memory of his mother dancing around in her nightgown with a glass of wine in one hand and a cigarette in the other began at age ten. Sometimes, she would cry; other times, she was angry. In either case, he would wind up at her bosom, giving her support. He remembered simultaneous feelings of conflict and excitement.

The illusion that Doug could save his mother was deeply rooted in his unconscious. He did not realize he was still twisted up in memories of his mother and trying to rescue her from self-destruction. Now, with women, he reenacted his hidden wish to save his mother and protect the little boy possessed with her seduction.

Until Doug faced the pain brought on by his conflicted arousal, he would not be able to break this pattern. He would have to grieve the absence of a healthy maternal presence and learn to relate to women who were self-sufficient and capable of healthy intimacy. Doug's last session was soon after he had met another woman twenty-five years younger than he, who was struggling financially, drank too much, and had a young child. He was not ready to face the fact that he could not heal anyone and then learn how to redirect this energy back to self-healing.

It takes courage and fortitude to admit that we unconsciously try to save people for all of the wrong reasons. A true friend can set boundaries, without trying to control anyone. Marcus said his moment of awakening happened when he received a note from neighbors that read "The drunk Marcus is not welcome in our home anymore. We love the sober Marcus, and he is always welcome." When his neighbors realized they were contributing to their friend's drinking problem, they changed their own behavior and set a loving boundary that helped Marcus face the truth about his alcoholism. Shortly after that, Marcus attended his first AA meeting.

If you are trying to fix someone else, you are the one who is broken. The miracle happens when we redirect healing back to ourselves and inspire change in others.

The Trapdoor

In addition to therapy and recovery programs, there are other avenues for the mind to heal. Freud stressed the importance of dreams as the "royal road to the unconscious." They hold a rich reservoir of unmined conflicts that can help lead you out of the maze. Your mind will gather events from your present life to create a story when you sleep. If you write down the dream as soon as you awaken, you can analyze the story to reveal an incomplete puzzle from your past. Do this regularly, and you will gain insight into your unconscious mind. Trust that your mind will only present what it is ready to heal.

Being still and allowing yourself to daydream can also bring up repressed memories. If memories start to surface, stay with them as long as they last. Journaling your feelings can help you to connect more deeply to your past. Do not forget that your discomfort is your road to healing; allow it to happen.

Remember that your templates and imprints are stored in your unconscious and drive you to repeat the same old patterns. When working with any type of relationships, whether they be couples, family, or groups, the templates and imprints of each person are explored. Until these grooves are identified, patterns remain locked in. Once revealed, individuals can depersonalize other people's actions and can provide more understanding and compassion of one another.

This first phase of learning about yourself and how your personality formed is essential to your growth. Recognizing that these painful memories are locked in a place beyond your consciousness is the beginning of healing them. One patient told me he did not want to remember his childhood pain; it was "like picking a scab." In reality, it is removing the splinter underneath the scab. Think of your wounds as the markers for the gold that lies beneath the surface of your mind. Rather than avoid those areas, dig deeply into those places so that you can mine the rich ore that lays dormant. Within that ore lies your wounds that are waiting to be converted into riches. Your mind wants to heal. Allow it to happen, and it will happen.

The following exercises will help you to identify your unconscious attempts to heal your past.

Moment of Reflection: Accessing Your Unconscious Reenactments

1. List the things that bothered or hurt you when you were young.

____

____

____

2. Did you feel like you could do something to make things better? If so, what did you try to do?

___

___

___

3. Do you find yourself attracted to people with similar personalities and issues? Describe the patterns that you have developed.

___

___

___

4. Are you willing to heal yourself first and only help those people in your life who truly want assistance?

___

___

___

5. Do you find yourself unwittingly copying your parent's dysfunctional behavior?

___

___

___

During the next week, write down your dreams and look for clues that might indicate old conflicts and wounds that are trying to surface.

Additional Journal Space

5

Chapter

Connecting the Dysfunctional Dots

> You can't connect the dots looking forward; you can only connect them when you look backwards.... You have to trust that the dots will somehow connect in your future.... Trust in something—your gut, destiny ... karma, whatever.
>
> —Steve Jobs

Thus far, we have learned that early events in our lives caused blocks in our personalities and kept us stuck in undesirable patterns. When we were young, a template formed that has functioned as a faulty navigation system, veering us in the wrong direction, time and time again. As stated in *A Course in Miracles*, we endlessly "search and never find." Recognizing that we are misguided, we can learn to follow a better path—one that will take us out of the maze. When we stop the harmful patterns, we can share and receive genuine love and spirituality.

Now that you have learned the origins of your unwanted behaviors, you can identify the common threads that have sabotaged your success. When you review your template and imprints and learn how this information was stored in your unconscious, you can connect the dots that governed self-defeating decisions.

Here is a brief review of your learning so far:

- Your template was formed based on your childhood experiences.
- Your imprints have impacted your romantic life.
- Templates and imprints can be compatible or collide.
- Your past, stored in your unconscious, governs you now.

Regardless of the form of the relationship, business or personal, your template will affect the outcome of your success or failures. When you understand your template, you have the power to heal and align your vision without sabotaging your success.

If They Can Do This, So Can You

Now that you've learned how the past has influenced your life, you've begun the journey of breaking old patterns. Many people have succeeded with this process, and so can you.

Through the learn, grow, and forgive process, Joshua was able to identify his template; with hard work, he broke through his unconscious barriers. He was raised in a southern town where family values were of the utmost importance. Church, loyalty, and staying in the family business were fundamental to acceptance. During high school, Joshua developed a fascination with the stock market and dreamed of going to Wall Street. In order to keep him in line with tradition, his parents refused to buy him books on investing or support his vision of success. His siblings made fun of his fascination with analytics, statistics, and profits and earnings ratios. Nevertheless, when Joshua graduated from high school, he saved money he made from the family business, and in spite of the resistance, he moved to New York.

At this point, his honesty, loyalty, and work ethic template paid off. Joshua was willing to do whatever it took to succeed. Hired at a brokerage firm, he swept floors, ran errands, got coffee, and did whatever was asked to make himself indispensable. Impressed with his eagerness to please, several of the brokers took Joshua under their wing and helped him to learn more about the trade. Confident of his future success, one of his bosses offered to lend him money for school and training.

As Joshua slowly moved toward his goal, his template was consistently challenged. He heard very little from his family, and when he went home for holidays, he felt shunned. His older brother referred to him as "Mr. Bigshot," and his father continued to ask him when he would be returning home to assist with the family business. The lack of family support created an ever-increasing sense of conflict and guilt. His unconscious guilt carried over to his current employment, slowing his progress up the ladder. Joshua was able to fulfill his education goals, but he was unable to achieve the financial success he wanted. His firm transferred him to Florida in the hopes that a different location would facilitate his progress, but this only further deepened his internal turmoil. He felt the same familial rejection of not fulfilling other people's expectations of him.

In therapy, Joshua had to learn how his family loyalty template was governing his current life. Though he had gone his own way, he carried the burden of unresolved unconscious conflicts. His depression lifted when he allowed himself to feel angry that his family held him back rather than allowing him to be his own man. He grew when he mourned the loss of his family and their support, and he recognized that it was not a religious conflict or family betrayal to honor his dreams; in fact, it was a testimony to both. He faced the reality that his family was not going to change, but he could still love them for the values they had instilled in him. His insights and healing created breakthroughs that allowed him to master his profession. The less guilt he felt, the more empowered he became, and he was able to chip away at his resistance and push through his internal barriers.

After a year, Joshua's firm offered to bring him back to New York, but he decided to stay with his current clientele. He had successfully created a new template of loyalty and trust, combined with financial and personal success.

Templates can be difficult to overcome, but when templates and imprints collide, the challenge creates the need for additional effort. As we discussed, similar backgrounds and romantic attractions can create insurmountable conflicts without conscious awareness and effort to bridge the gaps. However, templates and imprints need not align perfectly for a relationship to work. My husband, Skip, and I successfully navigated our own misalignment. Although I did not match his tall-blonde imprint, he did match mine: blue-eyed, tall, and distinguished. Our templates also were dissimilar. Skip was from a stable family with strong values. His father was a successful attorney and judge; his mother stayed home and took care of the children. He appreciated the stability his parents provided, but his extremely controlling mother created a pain template in him. He was not allowed to make decisions for himself. He was told how to dress, who to like, and so on. This pattern continued through college, humiliating him when she took it upon herself to redecorate part of his fraternity house. During his first marriage, Skip's mother attempted to insert the same influence, but he finally put a stop to it. As a result of this template, he recoils from any perceived feminine control, even if it is meant to be loving and helpful.

My childhood was quite different than Skip's. My parents were divorced when I was two. Though she loved me deeply, my mother worked at night as a nurse, which often left her too fatigued to care for me properly. My stepfather traveled and was unable to help. When he was home, he drank excessively and was abusive. His rage and sexual inappropriateness left a mark on me.

When Skip and I met, we had both been in therapy and experienced enough failed relationships to want a foundation built on friendship and trust. Though I thought he was handsome, I also thought he was wrapped a little too tight. Skip immensely enjoyed our conversations and time together, but the physical attraction was not immediate. As we spent more time with each other, our emotional attachment evolved into a strong physical attraction.

When I reacted, Skip's calm nonreactive demeanor allowed me to separate the present from the past. Instead of fueling my reaction with his wounds, he simply listened to me. When he reacted, he was open to hearing me remind him it was not his mother speaking to him. We lovingly discussed what triggered the conflicts and then laughed at ourselves. We discovered it was safe to be vulnerable with one another. As our relationship matured, a deep trust grew out of the closeness and respect we developed for each other. We were then able to enter marriage with a sense of security and the confidence that we possessed the elements for a successful union.

If these stories give you hope, be assured that you, too, can find success. By the time you finish this book, you will have the tools to actualize the life, including relationships, that you want. If you keep learning and growing through the parts that have prevented you from being a contented, happy person, you will succeed.

Leap of Faith

It is now time to sincerely ask yourself if you want to have a life out of the maze. If the answer is yes, then allow yourself to examine how your imprints and templates have governed your choices. Be willing to make this a lifelong process that keeps you moving into healthier patterns each time you use these steps.

In the following exercises, identify the themes of your past and assess how they are currently manifesting in your life. You will be taking your first step in walking toward a future that you can call your own.

Moment of Reflection: Connecting the Dots

1. How would you describe your early childhood template?

____

____

____

2. What is your imprint (physical preferences) in a partner?

____

____

____

3. The unconscious: what are you now doing that when you were younger, you swore you would never do?

____

____

____

4. In three or four sentences, how would you describe how your templates and imprints are unconsciously driving your unwanted behaviors?

____

____

____

5. Based on what you have learned so far, what patterns do you want to stop (addictive relationships, alcohol, codependency, drugs,

people-pleasing, excessive spending, unhealthy eating habits, gambling, procrastination)?

____

____

____

6. On a piece of paper, draw a maze describing how you have been stuck.

7. Now draw a map out of that maze, identifying the path going around the unconscious blocks into the direction you want to take.

8. Describe what you think your parents' (or caretaker's) childhoods were like.

____

____

____

9. Describe your ideal life and how you would like to see yourself in the future.

____

____

____

10. Now referring to your map, place the mile-markers of success and name your destination.

Additional Journal Space

Part II

Grow

6

Chapter

The Courage to Feel

> When you feel ... simply see it as energy passing
> through your heart ... relax and go deeper ...
> give room for the pain to pass through.
> —Michael Singer

Now that you've learned how imprints and templates have unconsciously dominated your behavior, it's time to take the next step and grow. The fundamental step to growth is to permit yourself to feel in ways that allow you to mature and spiritually evolve. If you do not feel, you will not heal; if you do not heal, you will stay in the maze. You will move further out of the maze each time you embrace your emotions and channel them in ways that empower you. You can do this.

First, you must recognize how unkind you have been to your emotions. You have done everything possible to eliminate your feelings. You may have ignored them, numbed them, stuffed them, or did whatever it took to distract yourself. Advertising has hypnotized us into thinking that abusing our bodies with deadly toxins is the way to feeling calmer or happier. Eat this food, take this pill, smoke this product; do anything to avoid your feelings. It is better to numb out than to pay attention to the feelings that might be emitting an internal warning. Alcohol, drugs, food, nicotine, and sugar are typical but ineffective ways to modulate emotions. The problem with this type of solution is that nothing ever changes. You do not learn, and you do not grow.

You can put this into perspective if you imagine yourself as a baby. Would you want your caregivers to give you a cigarette, a drink of vodka, or an injection of heroin to calm you down? Why in the world would you allow yourself to be brainwashed into doing these very things to yourself?

You must be careful not to treat your emotions like an enemy. After years of suppressing your feelings, they may be like frozen blocks of ice, trying to thaw during your healing process, and you must be willing to love yourself into emotional health. Sometimes, unexpected, intense emotions may pop up and cause you to feel out of control, but you are only out of control when you avoid these states. Suppressing feelings is like putting your finger in the hole of a dike. Either everything will come spewing out sideways or build so much internal pressure that the entire structure collapses.

Conversely, expressing highly charged emotions is like a lion roaring when all you needed to do was say, "Ouch." Neither underreacting nor overreacting produces healing communication. When we work through our emotions, we can speak in a manner that is productive and grounded in the present.

I Can Be Seen and Heard

It is entirely possible to feel peaceful most of the time. The mind has an incredible capacity to heal itself if you allow it to do so. Over time, it will naturally purge all pain and trauma through the ways we previously discussed: through sharing, through sobbing, and even through dreams. However, we often receive the message that it is unacceptable to express our emotions, especially men, for fear of appearing weak. Some adults tell children how they are supposed to feel and may even punish young people when they show anger or sorrow, rather than teach them how to express these emotions in healthy ways. Even worse, children with symptoms of anxiety, attention deficits, or depression are often put on brain-altering medications as a first protocol, rather than ruling out other factors by examining diet, psychological testing, or family therapy. These youth are labeled problematic and are conditioned to ignore and medicate their feelings at an early age. The template for a split in the personality ("I feel bad, but it's bad to feel") has already begun.

Sometimes, recovery programs unintentionally convey the message that we need to bypass our emotional healing. We should be more "cognitive and rational," be "grateful," or get rid of "resentments" and focus only on our own faults. Spirituality can be misinterpreted to indicate that if only we have faith, we would not feel bad. Failure to "rise above" weighs heavily on people unable to work through buried emotions, and that baggage prevents feeling connected to others or a higher power. True spirituality means that we do feel so that we can heal, and then we are real.

Growing Pain Is Good Pain

If you regard your feelings as the enemy, growing will be difficult because you will fight it every step of the way. You are not allergic to your feelings, and they will not kill you (unless you refuse to face and heal them). Our feelings are what propel us, and it is those same emotions that keep us trapped. Think about how often you have chased feeling good or ran from the bad feelings that might have helped you to make a positive change. This behavior is the root of all unbreakable patterns. You might be able to compartmentalize your emotions and get the illusion of feeling better, but the maze becomes only more expansive, and things only get worse.

If you have repressed your pain, it will continue to manifest itself under the disguise of new situations. A woman who was nurtured only during childhood illnesses might be frequently ill as an adult. A man whose mother was an alcoholic finds himself inexplicably attracted to emotionally broken women. A teenager who was told by his father that he would never amount to anything keeps sabotaging his success. A girl who was neglected and lonely in her youth later finds herself with emotionally unavailable partners. In these cases, people repeat and reenact the original wound template without any conscious awareness of how to stop. Old hurts lie dormant, festering and galvanizing new pain with old pain, and keep us going around and around in that emotional maze. You can heal your way out of the maze.

Face It and Embrace It

Sometimes, our emotions are unproductive reactions, but many times, they are warning signals, and our feelings must be validated. If we are suffering a loss, we need to grieve. If we are shocked or scared, we need to acknowledge these alarms. Our feelings can guide us like a barometer, to indicate a need for change. For example, if you feel taken advantage of and are depressed or resentful, this might signal the need to change the agreement you have with someone else. If you have suffered a loss, sorrow is a part of the grieving process. If you have been robbed or otherwise violated, an intense response to a real crisis is only natural.

However, in the absence of a crisis, whenever you react, remember that all of these responses are about the past. The current event is rubbing against on old, raw wound. Otherwise, the annoyance would be like water on a duck, and you'd be hard-pressed to remember the trigger a few hours later. If you want to empower yourself, you must use those reactive moments to heal the old and embrace a new way of self-expression.

Emotional healing is not an intellectual process. If you are going to grow, you must meet your emotions face to face, embrace them, and be still until they have neutralized. This simple process surpasses any other elaborate or sophisticated method of emotional healing.

Through Trapdoor # 1. Feel

There is a productive and gentle way to work through your emotions and steady your course. The way to grow through feeling is simple. We will call this your re-centering exercise. Just as a spinning top finds its center, you can learn to keep in balance when your mind is whirling. Permit yourself to feel.

First, recognize that whenever you are experiencing a strong reaction, it always has a taproot in the past.

Second, acknowledge that if you avoid feeling the original wound, you will only push new pain on top of old pain, causing the mind to obsess and expanding the maze.

Third, decide to be with your feelings; face them and embrace them.

Fourth, continue to go through these steps, and redirect your efforts on healing only yourself and no one else (unless they ask for help).

When a strong emotion pulls you into the vortex, embrace it. Lock in on the feelings (rather than the event), and allow them to surface without saying or doing anything. Whenever you feel the pain—or any other uncomfortable emotion—merely close your eyes and be still. Do not act out the feelings by doing or saying something. Allow the feelings to rise, and keep breathing. I repeat: breathe. If you feel angry, sit with it. If you feel scared, face it. If you feel sad, cry. We were given tears not only to cleanse our eyes but our hearts as well.

At first, you might feel flooded with memories and emotions, but at the end of the trail is peace. The old pain will feel like energy moving through your torso into your heart, where it will be purified and released. Then you will be able to accept the peace and joy that lay dormant underneath that old stockpile of pain. One patient described this process as a "volcano that erupted, spewing out all of my old anger and sorrow, and then a quiet space filled me with inexplicable compassion."

It might be difficult to believe this will heal all old wounds, but the key is to repeat this process every time a new reaction surfaces. Fear, fury, jealousy, shame: treat them like bubbles at the bottom of a glass of carbonated water. They float up and disappear. It is important to trust that every emotion will come up whenever it is ready, one at a time. Each release heals the heart and mind a little more. The secret is to continuously do this simple exercise as a natural part of your mental health. It takes but seconds each time to give yourself this gift.

After being married to an alcoholic for the third time, Jamie sought therapy because she "realized something was terribly wrong" with her judgment. She initially danced around her childhood, stating it was just fine. With gentle exploring and diligent journaling, her childhood memories and feelings surfaced, and she began to realize that things were not so great. Her father, though very successful, was a highly functioning alcoholic. He had been the owner of an automobile dealership, and the family had every material thing they wanted—except his attention. He was usually wrapped up in work or sipping on a cocktail. Jamie felt like she was missing him, even when he was in the same room.

As an adult, she had fun drinking with him, but that was the only connection they had. "No wonder I was always attracting emotionally unavailable men who were fun but shallow. I didn't know any better, and whenever I felt dissatisfied, I just ignored those feelings of boredom and frustration."

After Jamie's third divorce, everything crashed down on her. It was painstaking for her to review her childhood years. She lacked a close relationship with her father, and even worse, it was difficult to feel the painful memories she had worked so hard to avoid. As she learned how to journal her feelings, embrace them, and talk about her dreams, she slowly thawed. Once the tears started to flow, she feared they would never cease. Jamie grew to understand that this was a healthy grieving process, and she decided to stop fighting the pain. The more grief she released, the better she felt. More connected to herself, she began to attract men who were also emotionally available. When things did not work out, she was able to express her disappointment and move on. With time, Jamie began to love the life she had and all that it encompassed.

You grow when you begin to embrace your feelings. Our emotions are not meant to be squelched or medicated. When you give yourself time to journal, explore your innermost self, and talk openly, you are exposing the feelings and memories that need to be released. You must mourn disappointments and losses to renew yourself and clear the way for what life has to offer. Then, from a place of neutrality and feeling inwardly connected, you can form better attachments with yourself and others without dragging along your past. Let go of the pain, and let in the love.

Moment of Reflection: How Have You Dealt with Your Feelings?

1. What happened when you were angry as a child? How did you show (or hide) your anger?

___

___

___

2. Were you told it was okay to be angry?

___

___

___

3. What ways were you taught to express angry feelings?

---

4. What happened when you were sad?

---

5. Were you encouraged to cry and to release the sorrow, or were you told to stop crying?

---

6. Have you grieved the losses in your life? If so, how? If not, write down the reasons.

---

7. Do you recognize that grieving is a process of letting go of pain?

A Measure of Progress Exercise

Before you start this exercise, you will need a clear round vase and several sheets of red and black construction paper. The black paper will represent your current pain, and the red paper will symbolize your healing. Cut the black construction paper into about fifty strips, wad them up, and place them in the bowl. Then take some of the red construction paper and cut out fifty hearts about three inches in diameter and set them aside. (If you are artistic, be creative with this exercise.) Every time that you heal one of those bad feelings, or you feel good about something you have done, remove a piece of black paper and place a red heart into the vase. Take notice as your jar turns from black to red. In the following chapters, this exercise will be symbolic of how you are replacing fear and pain with love and hope.

Additional Journal Space

7

Chapter

Dismissing Dysfunctional Guides: Anger and Guilt

Every attack is a cry for love.
—*A Course in Miracles*

A Course in Miracles tells us that there are only two emotions: love and fear. Love is the voice of our spirit; fear is the message from the ego. The spirit is eternal love, which we are all born with; the ego is the headmaster of human-made rules; we follow to be accepted. We can learn to choose which voice we want to hear. One offers joy, the other pain. You will know which state you are in by whether or not you feel peace.

You were born a precious baby who was completely lovable simply because you existed. As you grew, maybe you were taught that there were certain conditions for being loved. You had to act a certain way, look a certain way, believe a certain way, or else you would not be loved. This programming causes our fear-based ego to tell us we can never measure up. We become fearful of loving ourselves and others because of the message we will never be enough. If we are taught to behave in loving ways, we will always be socially acceptable.

If we learn that all negativity comes from fear, we can enhance our healing process. Anger and guilt are the two negative emotions that serve as cover-ups for fear. They are the chief tricksters that hide our deepest fear: that we are not lovable. Anger and guilt are the main culprits for destroyed relationships. Anger (intimidation) and guilt (shame) are potent mechanisms for control and defense, but because they do not produce a win-win outcome, they are always dysfunctional guides. Real correction and strength come from facing these emotions. We move out of the victim or victimizer role when we learn to neutralize and then express these emotions in healthy ways. Only then can we find our way out of the maze.

We grow when we recognize that our ego's goal is to keep us in the maze until we are miserable and isolated. *The whole purpose of the ego is to digest our lives, one suggestion at a time.* It tells us to ignore our conscience. Goodbye, peace of mind. It tells us to eat or drink whatever we want. Goodbye, health. It tells us to lie and deceive. Goodbye, loved ones. It tells us to cheat. Goodbye, wealth. It tells us to put up with abuse. Goodbye, self-esteem. After the ego has caused us to fail over and over again, it tells us we can never be forgiven. It tells us we will not succeed. *When we give in or give up, the ego wins.*

The Ego's Thought System: The Maze

At Myself ← → **Anger** → ← At You

↑↓

It's My Fault ← → **Guilt** ← → It's Your Fault

↑↓

Stay Trapped

These ego-based patterns become embedded in our templates from childhood. Young children do not hold onto anger; they express it and move on. Children easily diffuse their feelings when they are acknowledged. Empathic responses such as "You feel frustrated that Billy doesn't want to play with you," "You're mad at me because I told you that you have to stay inside until you finish your homework," or "You're upset that Mommy and I were fighting last night" will usually soothe an angry child. When a parent's comments reflect a youngster's feelings and well being, the child's discomfort will naturally and quickly dissipate. When fear-based emotions are suppressed, the pain remains trapped in the child, who will later reenact those unresolved issues.

If children are not taught to talk out their anger and pain, they will self-medicate with substances or act out. Acting out anger takes the form of rebelling against family rules, breaking the law, drinking, drugging, cutting oneself, behaving promiscuously, or engaging in any other means of retaliatory, self-destructive behavior. When these patterns become habitual, the person remains trapped in an emotional cauldron, a constant state of depression, or a mixture of both. Addictive behavior is usually acted-out anger, while depression is anger turned inward. We can vacillate between both emotions. When we recognize the anger and guilt, and allow ourselves to experience them without acting on them, we reclaim the power to choose loving rather than anger or guilt-based decisions.

It might seem confusing to be told to embrace your feelings, yet now anger and guilt are called "dysfunctional guides." You can feel your feelings without acting them out. Think of your feelings as energy forces that pull you in different directions. Feeling and acting-out are not the same. When you react, you do not act; you sit back and neutralize. In other words, you make sure that you are calm before you express yourself. When you speak your truth from a place of love, change happens.

There are two different models to express feelings:

Something happens – React – Act out anger and pain – Blame or Withdraw

Something happens – Sit back, do not act, and re-center – Speak with love

The first model will create distance between two people; the second model will build intimacy and trust. Always remember to be neutral before you state your case.

Monica, one of the students in *A Course in Miracles*, shared how she learned that anger and guilt controlled her. She had failed to be a good mother because of her alcoholism. When she got sober and apologized to her children, ages eighteen and twenty, she thought things would get better. Her daughter was happy and supportive, and they were able to develop a close relationship. However, she felt a wall of resentment with her son. Monica told me, "I was always trying to please him, but no matter what I did, he often lashed out at me."

She felt his hostility most of the time, and she was angry that in spite of her efforts, their relationship did not improve. Monica offered to pay for family therapy, but he refused. When she started studying *A Course in Miracles*, she realized her ego was running the show. Guilt had kept her trapped in trying to make up for the past, something she could acknowledge but was powerless to change. "Anger and guilt," she said, "mostly at myself, meant I was forcing a relationship that was not meant to be at this time. I began to grow out of this pattern when I stopped allowing my reactions to govern me. I was able to accept that my son did not want the relationship I wanted, and that was okay. With love in my heart, I told him I was sad that we weren't closer, but we would both have to want a close relationship for it to materialize."

Monica recognized that she was not able to change her son's anger; that would have to be his choice. Regardless, she was able to find inner peace when she recognized that she could let go of her own anger and guilt. This freed both her and her son to follow their individual paths without being locked in an unforgiving state of anger and guilt.

Through Trapdoor # 2. Feel the Burn

As human beings, we tend to step on one another's toes, and it's only natural that we become angry when that happens. How we handle our anger can be either empowering or destructive. Anger is the burning emotion that the ego uses to convince us we need to take action, right now. When the ego fuels us with righteous indignation, it uses razor-sharp analytics to prepare the perfect case for annihilation. An overload of ramped-up passion renders facts irrelevant; releasing pent-up emotion is all that matters. Slamming on the horn for thirty seconds as opposed to a light tap serves no purpose. Screaming at a loved one for making an unconscious mistake only demoralizes the person—another lose-lose situation. Permanently cutting off a meaningful relationship is a sad solution to a temporary problem.

Anger starts as a small kindle that rapidly grows into a bonfire if the flame is not extinguished. Acting out anger only turns our fire on others – getting it out and acting it out is not the same. You can write out your anger, scream into a pillow, or talk to a neutral party, and then you can embrace your feelings without being overwhelmed. We must learn to sit with this feeling, lest we speak from a place of nuclear reaction. Instead, we wait until we are calm and then speak our truth. Allowing anger to neutralize is like smelting precious metals to refine them. Once the impurities are released from our emotions, we can communicate with clarity and kindness.

When someone is angry with us, we learn to receive the person with love and compassion rather than defensiveness or counterattack. If we feel attacked, we learn to say things like, "I can tell you're upset; let's both calm down and talk about this tomorrow. What's a good time?" This validates the other person's pain and diverts an overly heated discussion to a time when both people are calm enough to prevent hurting each other. *Waiting for the right time to communicate does not mean we avoid the discussion.* Following through means we will not sweep the problem under the carpet, for it later to reemerge with even greater force.

Healthy communicators honestly express their wants and desires, but they do not use coercion to obtain their goals. Two students in *A Course in Miracles,* Davin and Grant, give a beautiful example of healing communication. Grant had made an offhanded comment that unintentionally rubbed Davin the wrong way. At first, Davin felt a reaction, but after the surge of passion dissipated, he told Grant he needed to talk. Grant attentively listened as Davin told him he knew that Grant did not mean to hurt him, but Grant's comment reminded him of how his mother used to put him down. As soon as Davin expressed himself, he knew he had healed a wound from his past, and there was nothing to hold on to in the present. Grant also healed through his ability to hear his friend's feelings without defending himself. The poignant moment brought both people to a much deeper level of intimacy and trust.

Sometimes, requests are not honored because of ineffective communication. *You're supposed to know what my rules are* is the thought process of someone who thinks people are mind-readers. Expecting people do things a certain way without a mutual agreement is the ultimate form of manipulation.

If you are the target of someone else's anger, there is much you can do to avoid retaliation. *A Course in Miracles* teaches that "every attack is a cry for love." Because anger is a cry for love, we can respond with love. You do not have to smile at someone who is blasting you, but rather, you could say, in a warm and firm manner, "I want to hear what you have to say; please call me back when you feel calmer." You will show that you care without being pulled into a reactive mode. The presence of a therapist can help to neutralize the intensity of emotions and keep the focus on solutions. When facing a conflict, if our actions do not empower both people, the victory is lost. If we want to heal a burning situation, we must apply a balm of love and respect.

One couple, Martha and Daryl, learned to navigate their way through anger in a productive manner. As a child, Martha was screamed at when she did something wrong; thus, her template for guilt and frustration was rage rather than problem-solving. Daryl was slapped or spanked whenever he showed his anger, so he learned to escape negative emotions by shutting down. When Martha and Daryl had conflicts, she would rage, and he would stick his head in the sand, creating further distance in the relationship. By their first therapy session, they had stopped feeling any closeness and wanted to separate. When both recognized how they handled anger differently and became willing to learn a better way, the marriage improved. Martha made progress when she sat with her anger, remembered the pain that yelling caused her as a child, and then mourned those memories rather than reenacting them. Daryl found his lost childhood voice through journaling his feelings and then talking about them, even if it felt uncomfortable. Having embraced and neutralized their feelings, Martha and Daryl were able to address their conflicts and approach them from a place of mutual respect. After a few sessions, these former adversaries became friends, and love found its way back into their union.

The critical thing to remember about anger is that beneath it is the fear of not being loved. If we can recognize that every attack is a cry for love, we can respond in a way that bypasses this dysfunctional guide. Growing means reacting without acting until your turbulent emotions transform into loving words.

Through Trapdoor # 3. The Guilt-Trip Slip

Children are curious and should not be ostracized for making innocent mistakes. It is only natural for little boys and girls to test the rules of honesty, sexual conduct, and other inclinations, but if humiliated, they have a shame template for life. Children best learn when they are inspired to make the best choices. Taking the time to explain why certain choices are preferable to others helps a child to make good decisions.

Guilt rarely stops anyone from doing anything they were intent on doing, in spite of the shame. For example, a married person may feel extreme guilt for having an affair, but it doesn't stop the affair. A smoker may feel concerned about smoking, but the worse she feels, the more she smokes. A gambler is ashamed of his debt, but he only ups his bet. If guilt worked, we would stop the behavior the moment we felt guilty.

Unconscious guilt can be paralyzing and prevent you from living your life freely, governed through the ego's hidden marionette strings that want you to feel worthless and trapped. Racked with unconscious guilt, approval seekers make easy targets for exploitation and manipulation. Now is the time to stop following the advice of your ego.

Lynda recognized how she used guilt to control her husband. During her first session, she told me how her mother had taught her this very same behavior. Lynda's mother defined good and bad behavior by whether her requests were accommodated or not. Lynda did not want to be a bad daughter, so she would comply. This pattern continued into adulthood. Sometimes, her mother's demands created havoc in Lynda's daily schedule. Her mom would think nothing of calling Lynda at her law firm while she was preparing for a trial and asking her to run "urgent" errands. Trained on guilt, Lynda unconsciously reenacted the reversal of this theme in her relationships as well. Her husband was rarely at home, and she leveraged that against him when he would express concerns about her health as her weight increased. Lynda snapped back that food was her only source of nurturing, and then her husband would immediately clam up.

She sought therapy when she realized how she was emulating her mother. "I am using his absence to make him feel guilty," she said, "and as an excuse to eat whatever I want. Even worse, I didn't face the fact that my doctor repeatedly warns me that my weight is compromising my health. I can see that I am using food as a replacement for love. I'm now ready to do something about this so that I can feel better about myself."

There are many ways that people impose guilt to get what they want. Phrases such as "My sister's husband doesn't set limits on her spending" and "I wish I had a son like Mary Beth's; he always helps out his mother" are examples of this type of manipulation. Sometimes, coercion is as subtle as a look of dissatisfaction or disgust. One patient, Johnson, told me that for forty years, his mother controlled him with her facial expressions. If he did not do what she wanted, she would shrug her shoulders and have a downcast look on her face. Johnson would unconsciously feel so guilty that he would comply but would resent his mother for the manipulation. Later, when he realized he was people-pleasing at his own expense, he decided to change. He told his mother he was sorry that she was disappointed, but fixing her door right away meant being late to all of his other appointments. She stopped speaking to him for a couple of weeks, but then things improved. Johnson had to stay firm in his commitment to no longer be manipulated by his ego's urge to please his mother.

In healthy relationships, people accept no for an answer. People-pleasing to avoid conflict is the ego's tool to create inauthentic connections. This scenario causes feelings of devaluation and ultimately produces a lose-lose outcome: the ego's formula for separation.

A *Course in Miracles* teaches that rather than seeing ourselves as sinners, we should simply recognize our mistakes, which we need only to correct. When not consumed with guilt, it is easy to admit our mistakes, giving us more freedom to learn and grow.

I Don't Like It in Me, so I Blame It on You

Psychoanalysis and A *Course in Miracles* teach us that we often project our guilt onto others. When we accuse someone else of the very thing that we are doing, we are trying to alleviate our guilt by blaming that person. Recently, I had a patient who accused her husband of being financially irresponsible for buying a new car, shortly after she had secretly bought herself an expensive piece of jewelry. A person who is having an affair will attempt to alleviate guilt by coming home and finding fault with something in the house.

Projection is a classic defense mechanism in alcoholic marriages; you avoid your own actions by blaming your partner for drinking too much. I will never forget the middle-aged couple who sought marriage counseling and spent an entire session blaming each other for excessive drinking. As a condition for counseling them, I recommended that they both go to Alcoholics Anonymous for additional help. They stared at me with expressions of disbelief, shocked at my suggestion. Sadly, they did not agree with the recommendation, and I did not hear from them again.

Sometimes, life presents us with unfinished business from the past. Janice sought help because she could not get along with her stepdaughter, Lisa. She did not understand why Lisa thwarted all efforts to bond with her, and she felt rejected. She acknowledged that she was a good kid, but they could not get along. When I asked her if she ever had a stepmother, she said yes. After she told me about that relationship, she suddenly had a shocked look on her face. Janice was struck by the realization that her stepdaughter was treating her exactly as Janice had treated her own stepmother. After our session, she called her stepmother and apologized for all of the difficulties she had caused the family during her teens. Within a few months, Janice developed a loving relationship with her stepmother, and subsequently, her stepdaughter stopped acting out. Janice benefited greatly from recognizing the power of the unconscious and how to improve a current relationship by healing her past.

Instead of blaming someone else, we should learn to take a hard look at ourselves. Chances are, there is something in the present (or past) that makes us uncomfortable. Rather than being on autopilot and reenacting an unconscious event, you now have the power to take command of yourself and grow. You will always get closer to your goal when you act right rather than demand right.

Whenever you feel anger or guilt, do these re-centering exercises:

- Face and embrace your feelings.
- Close your eyes.
- Let the memories come.
- Breathe.
- Continue to feel the feelings.
- Stay connected until you feel neutral.

This is not a lengthy process. It should only take a few minutes. As soon as you have completed the process, briefly jot down what you learned and how you changed your behavior. Remember to repeat this process every time you are faced with the ego's tricksters of anger and guilt. As time goes on, you will move further and further out of the maze. You are growing.

Moment of Reflection – Retrace and Embrace Your Feelings

1. Do you use anger to get what you want from people?

___

___

___

2. How did your parents teach you to express your frustrations?

___

___

___

3. Has anyone made you feel guilty?

4. Did religion have a positive or negative impact on your self-esteem?

5. Have you made other people feel guilty to get what you want?

6. Has guilt kept you from feeling worthy to move into a better place?

7. List the ways that anger and guilt have prevented your movement in the direction of your deepest desires.

Additional Journal Space

8

Chapter

Shine Light on the Fear

Fear is never a reason for quitting; it is only an excuse.
—Norman Vincent Peale

Now that you've learned about the dysfunctional guides that have kept you from growing, you can learn about the one emotion that is the root of all others: fear. When you see how this single emotion has governed most of your thoughts and feelings, you'll be able to dismantle the force that has bound you. Once you do this, you can decide whether you want to stay in fear or make a choice for love instead. Imagine the personal empowerment you'll have when the rudder of fear no longer controls your destiny.

We can look at our chart again to see how fear hides at the root of all negative feelings:

The Ego's Thought System: The Maze

At Myself ← → **Anger** → ← At You

↑ ↓

It's My Fault ← → **Guilt** ← → It's Your Fault

↑ ↓

I'm Not Lovable ← → **Fear** ← → You're Not Lovable

Trapped in Pain

There Is No Love

Few people realize that fear controls most of their decisions and actions. Men, in particular, have been conditioned that it is unmanly to be afraid. Before you can ever master this driving force, you must stop using denial. It is not anxiety, discomfort, unwillingness, or any other label you have assigned. It is fear. By naming it, you now have the power to steer this energy in the right direction. Fear is the result of our ego thoughts based on the past. Something terrible happened, and we are programmed that bad things will keep repeating. We use all of our energy fretting over what is to come rather than saving that energy to assist us if something bad does happen.

According to the Anxiety and Depression Association of America, over forty million people have been diagnosed with an anxiety disorder in the United States alone. Many of these people are given medication to help them feel calmer. This programs you to believe that you are a helpless victim of your anxiety unless you take a prescribed drug. Medicine might help the symptom, but it is not a cure for the real problem. Remember that anxiety is just another name for fear.

The ego's purpose is to choose from fear and keep us separated and miserable, but we can choose otherwise. The ego continuously searches for evidence to support our sense of lack of love, money, safety, time—no matter how much we have. When we stop believing such things, we can eliminate the anxiety and panic that these thoughts promote. There is an abundance of love, money, safety, and time on this planet.

There's More Than One Channel to Watch

We learn to be fearful at a very early age. Adults can appear like scary, godlike giants in the eyes of vulnerable children. Caretakers program children to see themselves and the world in a particular way. If our template was painful and unsafe, we learned to fear the world as a threatening environment. Our family is not the whole world, and we can change the channel and learn to think for ourselves.

At the end of Charles's therapy, he told me that he was amazed at how fast his life was improving. "I thought all relationships were like my childhood," he said. "You had to think or act a certain way, or you would be rejected. Now that I recognize those fear tapes have been controlling me, I am free to think for myself and do what feels best to me. Already, amazing things are happening—a new job, sleeping better, more friends. All this simply because I'm listening to the voice in my head that says you can think for yourself and you can succeed—rather than the one that says, 'You better not try that.'"

Many of our life's choices come from fear rather than love. If we do not uncover this unconscious force and gather the courage to choose love instead of fear, we might make progress but will remain barricaded in the maze. Sometimes, the fear-wall seems too high or too long, but success is inevitable when we move through this invisible barrier. If fear is not our guide, we are free to venture out into a different world, one that offers love. Unless you want it to, fear no longer controls you.

Red Lights Are Good Lights

Sometimes, you get confused between your fears and your intuition. Fear is often based on imaginary thoughts rather than facts. Your intuition is a built-in natural guide that cautions against real danger. It warns you about such things as walking out in front of a car or making a bad decision. Fear can prevent you from acknowledging and embracing your highest aspirations and lead you to settle for less. Ego-driven fear stops you from growing; intuition leads you to success. If you are confused, you can ask yourself if what you are doing is in the highest good of everyone involved. If the answer is yes, you are making a loving choice. Sometimes, it might seem that your decision will hurt someone. For example, if you consider ending a relationship, you might think it's better to stay than to cause another person pain. There is nothing loving about being with someone you do not want. When you set yourself free, you also set the other person free to grow and find true love. It is never too late to reconnect to your own inner source of guidance and truth; in fact, your happiness depends upon this.

The Boogie Man Is in My Head, Not under the Bed

Most of us have childhood memories of scary shadows and other uninvited guests in our bedrooms at night. Some of those ghostlike figures continue to lurk in our minds; they feel very real, even though they are not. Mark Twain's famous quote, "I've had a lot of worries in my life, most of which never happened," could not state this better. We need to face our fears so that we can see that most of them are not real, and even those that are real can lose their grip on us.

Fear that keeps us from facing our sorrow and grief will keep us bound in pain. Fear of being alone causes some people to settle for unsatisfactory relationships. Fear of exposing unwanted parts of oneself causes someone to end relationships and even therapy abruptly: "If you know the real me, you will reject me, so I will leave before that happens." Many people run away from those who care about them because they are afraid of getting too close—the very thing they crave. All of this boils down to fear of the unknown. Some may hate their lives, but when asked how they are benefitting from staying the same, they admit they simply do not like change. They learned to live with the ghosts, believing they are not as scary as the unknown.

For some, being loved is the scariest feeling of all. The fear of commitment might mean feeling swallowed whole or risking unbearable rejection. Bernadette, terrified of relationships, told me, "I was an only child and a lonely adult. Alcohol and cigarettes became my closest companions. I did not think I would ever be able to stop. When I finally did get sober, I was terrified to give up smoking. I prayed for the willingness to quit, and at two years sober, I succeeded. At first, it was hard, but with each passing day, the genuine love that I received from people far exceeded the deadly comfort from any addictions."

Some people become controllers out of fear. *A Course in Miracles* teaches us that when we are trying to control, we compete with God. We must admit that we have no say over how the universe operates. We do have the power to make personal decisions about our behavior, but when we try to manage other people, we will be as successful as tugging on a plant to make it grow or demanding the sun take a different orbit.

Sometimes, we fail to make progress toward our goals because we are not aware of fear. In therapy, we call this resistance, and it shows itself in the form of inaction. When someone is given an assignment and does not follow through, or when a patient is not honest, forgets appointments, or will not commit, unconscious fear is at work. Resistance prevents a person from growing. Again, Mark Twain put it best when he said, "Courage is resistance to fear, mastery of fear, not absence of fear." In daily life, resistance shows up when we do not take action for what we want, usually under the excuse of lack of money or time. Like anger and guilt, money and time are cover-ups for fear.

Now Is the Only Time There Is

Fear of the future, based on the past, is another wall that we must overcome if we want success. Those who are paralyzed by fears of the past must realize it is never too late to write new scripts. In group therapy, Herman describes this heart-wrenching story about his fears of having children: "When I was seven years old, I was with my parents and my little brother at a park. My parents wanted to go to the bathroom, so they sat us by a fountain and told me to watch my little brother. When they came out, we couldn't find my brother; he'd fallen into the water and drowned. They screamed at me and told me I had killed him. My life took on a permanent horror with this declaration. I decided that I could never be trusted or responsible for anyone again."

This tragedy scarred Herman for most of his life until he learned that he was not the one at fault. A seven-year-old is not capable of being responsible for a younger child. Once Herman realized that his parents had made the mistake, he was able to replace fear with understanding and self-forgiveness. Herman was willing to tell his secret, feel the shame it caused, and relive the pain of an unbearable tragedy. He was terrified to re-experience this horrible memory, but by having the courage to do so, he released himself from the prison of a lifelong sentence of guilt.

Through Trapdoor # 4. Fear

Years ago, I was enrolled in a personal growth course in Fiji that offered several assignments to help us overcome fear. One of them involved jumping off a bridge on a moonless night. On the bus ride to the drop-off, all I could think about was the time I was snorkeling in the Bahamas and witnessed a huge tiger shark that bumped the underbelly of another unsuspecting diver. I watched in horror, sure that my heartbeat was so loud it was signaling me as live bait. Fortunately, my dive partner guided my paralyzed body back to the boat, and the three of us made it out of the water before the predator returned for another taste. Reliving this terrifying event on the way to the bridge made me question whether I'd be able to perform the task ahead of me. When it was time to jump, I was shaking so violently I had to be lifted onto the railing. Then without delay, I said a short prayer, asked for courage, took the hand of my partner and jumped. After we hit the water, our hands were separated, and I panicked, feeling all alone with my fear.

At that point, I had to decide to endure the terror and embrace it. After several minutes, the horrifying images of sharks circling underneath gave way to the beauty all around me. There were only the blackest black and twinkling lights in the sky, and I could not tell if I was in the water or the heavens. Nothing mattered but the fact that I was a speck of life floating in an endless universe. Much later on shore, I felt an exhilaration of self-trust never before experienced—a new metaphor for walking through my fears.

Find the Light

A *Course in Miracles* teaches us that there is no problem that trust will not solve. When we trust that there is divine order in our lives, we approach our problems with a willingness to grow and learn from our fears. This decision to trust is the light that will cause our fears to lose its power over us. When you choose to embrace life, even when you feel overwhelmed with fear, you will empower yourself, and life will keep getting better. Only when we avoid the discomfort does it follow us around.

As before, here are the re-centering steps to work through your fears:

- Face and embrace your feelings.
- Close your eyes.
- Let the memories come.
- Breathe.

- Feel the feelings.
- Stay connected until you feel neutral.
- Do the exercises at the end of this chapter.

Remember to do this each time you are unable to move forward, and stay connected until you have accessed old pain or messages. Allow yourself to feel whatever fears arise. Remember that growth depends on you being able to feel and release your fear.

Patty was diagnosed with anxiety when she was twenty years old. At times, she found she could barely breathe, and her heart raced so fast, it terrified her. When she went to the doctor, he told her she was suffering from anxiety and prescribed valium. He never explored the causes of her panic or suggested counseling as an alternative to pills. Patty got in the habit of using valium every time she felt anxious, and she eventually became addicted. When the valium didn't work, she formed another dependency on alcohol. This vicious cycle continued for the next twenty years until Patty landed in treatment for chemical dependency. She was so accustomed to taking something for her fear that she was resistant to alternative methods such as relaxation and meditation. In therapy, she would be angry at me for encouraging her abstinence rather than directing her anger at the physician or pharmaceutical companies who promoted her addiction in the first place. After several relapses, Patty was willing to learn that her anxiety started in childhood when she was sexually abused. She had blocked this memory, but it resurfaced whenever she felt trapped. Patty grew when she allowed herself to feel her anxiety and heal her painful memories without using drugs to blot them out.

We must face the fact that if we want to receive something, we must also give up something. If you are on a sinking ship and want to be saved, you either jump in the lifeboat or sink with the ship. Now is the time to let go of things that have steered your life to nowhere. Now is the only time you have.

By mastering your fear, you can turn your negative energy into positive energy so that you can grow. The following exercises will help to clarify this for you. You may feel uncomfortable at first because your ego does not want you to get out of the maze. But if you arc willing to open your mind and try these exercises a few times, you will be encouraged by the new source of strength that gradually replaces your fear with the beauty of self-love.

Moment of Reflection: Facing the Fear

This exercise is designed to expose the fear underneath all of your negative emotions.

1. I think I'm anxious about ____________, but I am really afraid of ____________________. For example: I think I'm anxious about my health, but I'm really afraid of death.

Now list yours:

____

____

____

Instead of choosing fear, I choose to

____.

For example: Instead of choosing fear, I choose to take good care of myself, get a medical check-up, eat right, exercise, and accept my mortality.

2. I think I feel guilty about ______________, but I am really afraid of ____________________.

For example: I think I feel guilty about an affair I had in my first marriage, but I'm really afraid of being punished.

Now list yours:

____

____

____

Instead of choosing fear, I choose to

____.

For example: Instead of choosing fear, I choose to heal my past, make amends, learn from my mistakes, and forgive myself.

3. I think I am angry about _______________, but I am really afraid of _______________.

For example: I think I am angry about my son's disrespect toward me, but I'm really afraid we will never be close. I'm also afraid this might affect his other relationships as well.

Now list yours:

____

____

____

Instead of choosing fear, I choose to

____.

For example: Instead of choosing fear, the next time my son is disrespectful, I choose to lovingly tell him that I would like him to talk to me in a kind manner and that I am worried if he's disrespectful to other women, they or himself won't respect him.

4. I think I am reluctant to ______________, but I am really afraid of ______________.

For example, I think I am reluctant to lose weight (quit smoking, quit drinking), but I am really afraid of how I will feel when I stop.

Now list yours:

____

____

____

Instead of choosing fear, I choose to

____.

For example: Instead of choosing fear, I choose to recognize that something is attempting to destroy me by hijacking my mind. I can replace these false comforts with real love.

5. Make a list of the things you are not happy about and what you would like to change.

____

____

____

6. Take an honest inventory of how you resist working through your fears and write them down.

____

____

____

7. Circle the things you are willing to do when you are afraid.

Identify the fears rather than avoid them.

Identify the thoughts that create the fear.

Face and embrace my feelings.

Choose courage rather than avoidance.

Develop a plan that outlines the steps to replace the fear with new behavior.

8. Are you willing to take new risks rather than being imprisoned in your fears?

Make it a habit of doing these exercises every time a fear controls you.

How many red hearts do you have in your jar?

Additional Journal Space

9

Chapter

Freedom from Bondage

Let there be space in your togetherness, and let the
winds of the heavens dance between you.
—Kahlil Gibran

In healthy relationships, sharing and receiving love is natural. When our neediness causes us to caretake unwilling participants, we are not offering love at all; we only keep ourselves in the pain maze. Fear of being alone, financial insecurity, or the need to feel in control are unhealthy motives and unconscious reenactments. When we try to control others, we avoid our own healing, all the while causing guilt and resentment in the other person. The parent who tells the adult child how to live, the loved one who rescues rather than allowing consequences, and the partner who focuses on fixing the other for selfish motives are examples of fear-based helping that only keep us in bondage. Now is the time to lovingly change yourself.

Freedom from bondage means we release ourselves and others as hostages from emotionally unhealthy relationships. We replace fear with love and stop trying to control anyone or anything, including ourselves.

Healthy Parent, Healthy Child

Parents often panic as they watch their addicted child spin out of control. There is nothing more horrifying than seeing your beloved son or daughter engage in life-risking behavior while feeling powerless to help. Often, possessed by the dysfunctional guides of anger, guilt, and fear, parents will do all of the wrong things in the name of helping. The greatest love a parent can give a child is to be mentally healthy.

As hard as it is, families that stop enabling children by giving them money, legal support, and shelter have the greatest success in helping their offspring. When parents stay out of the way and disengage from the problem, children are forced to face the consequences of their choices. Love is never withdrawn. Instead, we remove the deadly support that keeps the child sick. We stop bailing people out of their difficulties. We replace enabling with love by telling children how much we care, and that is why we will not rescue them anymore. When the person can no longer manipulate and runs out of money and options, a willingness to get better will be born. It is then we can offer help.

David and his wife, Tanya, were referred for therapy because they were too preoccupied with work and their social lives to give their son, Greg, the attention he needed. To assuage their guilt, they gave him plenty of things but not enough quality time and support. At age thirteen, he started hanging around with drinkers and drug users. Greg stopped coming home at night and then went missing for days while his parents frantically searched for him. They tried everything to control him: restriction, therapy, taking away the car—but things only got worse. He flunked out of school. "We don't know what to do," David said. "He sleeps all of the time, and when awake, he is resentful and angry. We thought of kicking him out of the house, but we are afraid we might lose him forever or that he might die on the streets."

As part of therapy, David and Tanya were referred to Al-Anon for parents of addicted children so that they could learn to redirect their efforts back to themselves. They learned how to "detach with love" and told their son they cared too much to stand by and watch him destroy his life. They established rules for Greg. He had to stop using alcohol and drugs and get therapy, or he would have to move out. When he did not follow through, they gave him a week to find a place to live. Greg moved in with a friend, but after two weeks, he was asked to leave. When he begged to come back home, his parents agreed on the condition he followed the rules. At first, he refused. His parents had a harrowing three weeks of silence, but Greg finally called to say he would do anything. As a young man, his recovery was fast. Three months sober, he earned his GED, got a part-time job, and enrolled in the community college. His parents still go to Al-Anon, continue therapy with their son, and are healing as a family. Greg was fortunate that his parents dared to change themselves and to love him into wellness.

Romantic Roller-Coaster Ride

The love addiction is the most difficult of all romantic relationships. Some couples enjoy dancing on the edge of the cliff; they play out their insecurities in a false love affair. They share a sense of excitement through crazy playfulness, intense love-making, and a mental twist not duplicated with anyone else. They fill an intensity in each other that makes other people seem boring. Unfortunately, the downside of their joyride is that all the things that make the relationship fun and exciting also make it deadly. The best they bring out in each other is accompanied by the worst. Thus, the positive bonds they share are corroded by anger, fear, and unpredictability. When they are unable to replace the intensity they share, they reconcile with abandoned passion, temporarily forgetting all the mutually inflicted pain. They resolve nothing, and the bondage pattern is destined to repeat again and again.

Jonathan came to therapy for help with his addictive relationship. He met Susan in a nightclub. They clicked right away; although something inside of him said, "Danger," it only made the encounter more exciting. When they kissed, he felt a magical connection. She was sensitive and vivacious, never boring. He told me he never had so much fun with a woman. After three heavenly months, the relationship became "crazy," and she would break up with him for minor grievances such as not texting her enough, or being five minutes late. "When I did not call her three times a day," he recalled, "she would imagine I was with someone else and would block my calls." The rejection was unbearable, and he could not quit thinking about her. Eventually, she would unblock him, and they would plunge back into sexual bliss. Things would be okay for a week or two, and then the pattern would begin anew. "I felt like I was going insane, and my friends told me I needed to be committed."

In therapy, Jonathan recognized that Susan awakened in him an aliveness that he had never experienced. Before meeting her, his life was all work and no play, and she rocked him with excitement. For the first time, he had a playmate that helped him to forget everything else. He learned the newfound spontaneity in him would remain and realized that the fun and romance with Susan could happen with other people as well. He had to learn the difference between love and pain, and stop confusing the two. He grew when he mourned his painful childhood template and learned that loving relationships are comforting, not traumatic. He started a bucket list—golf, cooking, and dance lessons—and opened up a new world for himself. He made new friends so that all of his emotional eggs were not in one basket.

All You Need Is Me

Codependency happens when a person's energy focuses on changing someone else. Such people would sell their souls and do anything to protect their own interests. Codependents are under the unconscious fantasy that they are just caring and will be happy if the change occurs elsewhere—an illusion that keeps on giving. Even if the other person does change, the codependent will seek a new situation or person on which to focus. By locking onto people who represent an unhealed past, the codependent attempts to re-engineer the past, by manipulating the present.

Codependency means getting a good feeling about yourself by focusing on another's problems, a way of replacing real help (love) with harm (fear). We act from love when we help people to help themselves. We act from fear when we don't allow people to find their own way to happiness. For real change to occur, the desire must come from within us. We cannot make people see what they refuse to see or do what they refuse to do. We can set boundaries and conditions to enable someone to receive help, but only with a willing participant. Love facilitates the healing process. "It waits on welcome, not on time," teaches *A Course in Miracles*, but love does not force itself where it is not wanted.

Rebecca recognized her pattern of forming codependent relationships with emotionally unhealthy men. "If I like someone," she said, "I want to attach myself to him. If he pulls away, I will try harder, do more … to gain control of my anxiety. I lose myself in trying to please so that he will do what I want—quit drinking, grow up, treat me right, etc. None of this has worked. Most men avoid my web and want to flee. Ironically, the ones who are comfortable in the trap, I don't want. I finally realize who needs to stop the addiction, and it's me. I am the one who needs to grow up."

I Want Out; I Can't Let Go

Locked-in dependence exists when both people bond in a way that shuts the door to growth in their relationship. These provisional relationships last out of fear of being alone, of making mistakes, for financial reasons, or fear of the unknown. They may have been dissatisfied for many years, but neither person is willing to rock the boat, risk failing, or venture out of the perceived safety net. Often, one or both will turn their backs on the infidelities of the other, just to keep things copacetic. As the years pass, the gap widens, but they cling to the scraps of their relationships through children, financial interests, or whatever keeps them together. This duo may spend a lifetime of settling; in some cases, one may find new love elsewhere.

Derrick came to see me because he was in pain after the ending of an extramarital affair. He said he loved his wife and thought very highly of her, and he could not imagine getting a divorce. She was attractive, intelligent, a good mother, a good friend, and well-liked in the community, but the passion was long gone. She was not interested in his attempts to rekindle the flame. He had felt lonely for many years. He had numerous affairs, and his guilt blinded him from the reality that both he and his wife deserved to be happy. His last affair began when his wife no longer wanted to have sex. When that affair ended abruptly, the rejection sent him reeling into "uncontrollable pain." He admitted he found great pleasure through classical music, charity work, and his grown children, but now his loneliness and despair prevailed. He said he wanted a real emotional connection with a woman with whom he could share the deepest parts of himself. Derrick was not willing to be alone to wrestle with his dependency demons and face his fear. After several months of therapy, he remained unable to commit to the learning and growing necessary to change his pattern. His unresolved guilt, dependency, and fear kept him in bondage. Unable to fully explore the reasons for his overdependent marriage, he could not find a deeper intimacy or allow the love for his wife to change from marriage to friendship. Derrick sentenced himself to a life of silent suffering.

It takes great courage to learn, grow, and forgive. I have learned to respect the choices of my patients, even if it means they stay in the maze. Though uncomfortable to witness, it is not my place to judge. It is better to acknowledge the progress they have made rather than focus on what they are not ready to grasp.

I Am All I Need

Anti-dependency can result when there is so much neglect that children go through life relying on no one but themselves. These individuals might be incapable of the vulnerability needed for healthy attachments. When you try to bond with someone who is anti-dependent, you will encounter an emotional wall.

Brunswick saw marriage as an "unsatisfying merger," but he wanted to understand the components of a healthy relationship. He learned that his template developed into self-sufficiency during his lonely, solitary childhood. Relatives and babysitters raised him, and he was sent to boarding school in the sixth grade. He received the message that he was too big of a bother for his parents. Sadly, he often wondered why he had ever been born. He conformed to the structure of boarding school, but not without feeling abandoned by his parents.

Once Brunswick was willing to embrace the truth of his lonely and independent childhood and do the work of learning, growing, and forgiving, he was able to open himself to healthy bonding. He learned that connections are the result of mutual openness and trust. His most significant growth occurred when he made specific requests if something bothered him, or when he recognized he needed help and asked for assistance. As his growth continued, he was able to enjoy emotional intimacy with his partner without forfeiting his independence—friends, hobbies, and interests outside of the relationship.

Another patient, Marsha, started therapy because she was depressed. Marsha, an only child, had been sexually abused by her uncle and had never been married. Her adult romances were superficial and fleeting. Her current relationship was with her prior (married) therapist, with whom she reenacted her childhood sexual abuse. When Marsha unconsciously came on to her therapist, he was seduced by her rather than helping her to understand her pain template with her uncle. Marsha was still entangled in this affair when she came to see me.

In therapy, Martha would offer gifts, and when I would ask her to explore this, she would feel rejected. She was trying desperately to bond yet struggled to find a balance. She felt therapeutic boundaries were punitive rather than protective. It was my fears that thwarted my struggle to help Marsha achieve balanced dependence and intimacy. I constantly reminded her of "appropriate boundaries," without allowing a natural closeness to develop. I was trained that therapists must always maintain an objective distance, but this created an unnatural atmosphere in sessions. Her anti-dependent personality served her well. She was able to stay in therapy regardless of the rejection she felt. She stopped drinking, grieved her abusive childhood, and made peace with her past. She was able to break her seductive pattern with men, though she never found the relationship she said she wanted.

As I've matured as a therapist and as a person, I've often reflected on my time with Marsha. By keeping her at arm's length and not understanding my own fears and frustrations, I kept her from experiencing a healthy dependency with me. When she would ask me questions, I would ask her to analyze why she wanted to know, rather than being sensitive to her desire to feel closer. When she would tell me that I didn't understand how she felt, my anxiety about her feelings caused me to babble about transference rather than do the deeper work—the longing she felt for a mother. She perceived herself as bad because of my own emotional unavailability and insecurity—a re-enactment with her mother that could we were unable to break. Fortunately, personal healing has taken me out of this maze. The work is much richer and the process much faster when both the therapist and the patient are willing and able to do the work together. I no longer feel it is wrong to love a patient, as a mentor, healer, and a person who can be trusted.

When we are afraid of losing someone, and we try to manage that person, our fear squeezes the love out of the relationship. Whether it be children, friends, relatives, or lovers, we cannot hold on too tight, lest the other be compelled to wiggle out of our grasp. Even if we succeed at controlling someone, there is a price to pay. The relationship becomes dull and mechanical, lacking revitalization. The delicate balance of too little versus too much can be like a fine violin—beautiful music comes from the right tuning and timing. Love is complete; it does not control and always basks in the joy of freedom and self-expression.

We Need Each Other

Loving relationships consider the needs of both participants. There is an interdependency with a balance of mutual reliance. At times, one person gives more than the other, but no one is keeping score, and things always balance out. In these healthy relationships, both people are mindful of giving and receiving, at times merging as one, and then allowing for individuation to recharge. There is empowerment in supporting each other's growth. Healthy relationships enable a bond to form while modulating insecurities when they arise. We do not fear separations, because we have learned the root of our fears and grown from them. We meet our reactions with the desire to heal the past, without projecting them onto those we love. We share what triggers us, but only to be more visible and real to those around us. Through sharing our inner core, we feel close and comfortable with intimacy and vulnerability. The request for an opinion brings an honest, loving answer. We share our true feelings without demanding change in another.

Conflict Is the Bridge to Success

Conflict is not the stopping place; it is the bridge to success. Almost everyone wants to run for the hills whenever conflict surfaces. However, this means fear wins, and the conflict backpacks right along with you into your next relationship. When conflicts are approached without blame, the needs of all are considered. One evening, a student in the *Course in Miracles* shared that a girlfriend once told him, "I love you very much, but this behavior just doesn't work for me." He said she did it in such a loving way; he was able to laugh at himself. Through this type of commitment to honesty in our relationships, we find the deepest bonds of a genuine, loving connection.

Candace told me she wanted to stop group therapy. When I asked her why, she said she was ready to "just have fun," that she had learned enough, and could continue to heal alone. In the same breath, she told me she felt that one of the group members didn't like her. When I asked her if she might be running from her feelings, she told me, "It is crystal clear to me that I should just live my life and have fun. I can continue *grow*ing without the group." I reminded her that anything that is crystal clear during a conflict is undoubtedly the advice of the ego. Was it possible the member she thought disliked her was opening a throbbing wound? Maybe this perceived enemy was offering her a gift of healing?

Candace did not like what I said, but she was willing to concede the possibility. She then told me that the group member reminded her of a kindergarten classmate who made fun of her—devastating to her already-fragile ego, causing further withdrawal into her shell. Candace returned to the group and shared why she had not been attending. Her intuition was right; the other group member admitted that Candace reminded her of the sister, the favorite of her parents, prettier and smarter than she. By getting to the roots of their conflict and facing the tension, they were able to meet each other in the here and now. With much tears and laughter, they embraced with newfound camaraderie and love.

Relationships feel good until they get real. If Candace had walked away from the group, she would have missed the golden opportunity presented to her. As *A Course in Miracles* says, "Your enemy is your gateway to heaven." Both Candace and her former antagonist found heaven when they used their conflict as a healing instrument to get out of the maze.

Let Go and Grow

Guilt, and fear of lack are at the root of unfulfilled dependencies that create bondage, not love. We must let go of these dysfunctional guides if we want to grow. The ego uses guilt, feeling that you are unforgiven and don't deserve better, and fear that there's a lack of potential partners, in order to keep us stuck in the maze. *A Course in Miracles* teaches us that relationships will last as long as there is growth. Once the connection has provided the maximum amount of learning, then love only changes form. In other words, there is no loss, just a different type of love. When we are full of love, we do not fear abandonment because we know that we can still love the same person—only differently. The tree lets go of the acorn; the acorn changes form and grows into a tree and then produces more acorns. Love is forever changing and expanding. If we remember to love in the present moment rather than in the past or forever, we would be free of the dependence that creates a loveless relationship.

Perhaps you see some parts of all these situations in yourself. Relationships are the learning centers for growth, the meat of all existence, and sometimes additional help is needed. Engaging a psychoanalyst trained in working through difficulties can greatly facilitate this process. It takes commitment to keep facing oneself, matched with equal commitment by the therapist to help you with resistance. At times, it seems like too much work, and both people feel like giving up. Skilled psychotherapists can work through their own negative transference while helping you to keep your goal intact. Remember that learning, growing, and forgiving is forever a process of accumulating more and more success. Now is the time to attract relationships that offer love and freedom to be yourself.

Moment of Reflection: Relationship Review

Think back on your relationships (friends, family, and lovers) as you contemplate the following questions:

1. What were the most significant relationships when you were young? In what ways were they satisfying? In what ways were they dissatisfying?

____

____

____

2. As an adult, do you see those same patterns showing up?

____

____

____

3. Are you comfortable with the ebb and flow of your relationships? Do you hold on too tight? Not tight enough?

____

____

____

4. Are you willing to be intimate (share your true self) with someone and encourage your loved one to be open with you?

5. Describe in your own words what a healthy relationship looks like.

6. Take a moment to describe your ideal friendships, family relationships, and romantic relationships. What do you like best about how you show up with these people? What would you like to do differently?

7. Are you willing to face and heal the conflict with the people in your life? If so, how will you do this when you feel uncomfortable?

8. How full is your jar of hearts?

Additional Journal Space

10

Chapter

Freedom from Pain

Perfect love casts out fear. If fear exists,
then there is not perfect love.
—*A Course in Miracles*

Now that you know how the dysfunctional guides of anger, guilt, and fear have kept you in bondage, you can also see how love has been confused with pain. The short-term discomfort of facing the pain is well worth the healing that you will gain, but beware. Once you release yourself from bondage, the ego will try to lead you from one pain trap to the next.

I believe that the most undiagnosed addiction of all is the addiction to pain—the need to feel something rather than nothing; the reason we move in and out of the pain. Most individuals trapped in the pain maze have become conditioned to self-medicating their suffering and feel bored, depressed, and restless when things seem normal. One patient, stuck in an addictive relationship, told me, "My relationship is crazy—things are either really good or really bad, but I keep going back because I can't stand to be alone." Another patient, though once prosperous, now alone and lonely, lost his wealth as a result of an adult child who manipulated him out of his wealth. A gentleman I saw had an abusive employer, but his financial insecurity kept him stuck in his job. Almost every substance abuser I have worked with relapsed because they did not like the way they felt. All of these individuals were afraid to let go of a bad situation in exchange for a more loving existence. Only by freeing ourselves from these demoralizing attachments are we able to grow. The desire to learn how to love yourself must be stronger than the desire to self-destruct.

To Have It, Give It Away

To receive love, you must be love. When I was in my healing process and seeking truth, everything was paradoxical and confusing. It seemed that every time I learned one thing, the opposite lesson presented itself. I needed to be in a relationship only after I knew how to enjoy living alone. I needed to be unselfish and giving, yet had to be selfish and learn how to receive. I needed to be willing to love with complete commitment yet let go in a flash. I had to be open to love, but not from a place of need.

Not until I experienced a profound spiritual meditation was I able to unravel my confusion. One night, while meditating, with eyes closed, I saw a ball of white light as if inside my forehead. It looked like a beautiful bright moon, and when I strained to experience it more fully, the globe of light shrank away. The harder I tried to recapture it, the smaller it became. For many months, I attempted to comprehend that experience.

Over the years, I grew to understand this powerful moment in my healing. The light was love, and in my state of calm communion with my spirit, it came to me, unexpectedly and naturally. I only had to allow that light to shine to receive the comfort it transmitted. Nothing else was required. In real life, when I was searching, love moved away. This meditation showed me that love is not something that I need to find, because its presence is always within me. I need merely to be quiet, let go, and receive the light that is a natural part of my being. This empowering awareness left me with a certainty I was never truly alone. I was the one who kept myself in a fishbowl.

When an unhealed mind sets out to find love, it inevitably will fail; it's more likely to attract another wounded soul. Without a commitment to love, the ego will discover reasons to undermine the relationship. A healed mind will attract people who also are capable of genuine love. These relationships are entirely different from those built on unresolved pain and fear. Now is the time to consider converting all the pain in your relationships to healing and love.

Curveball, Home Run

When you are accustomed to medicating your feelings with an addiction, it is only natural that you will feel a new kind of pain when you stop. The pain that was covered up did not go away; it simply hid—unexpectedly overwhelming you, unconsciously drawing you back into the behavior you want to stop. The pattern starts with feeling sick of the adverse effects of the addiction, then stopping, then forgetting about the sickness, feeling uncomfortable, then starting again. The ego takes charge and tells us, "It will be different this time." We do not question this, the impulse to feel differently overrides all else and back in the maze, we go. If you want to heal forward, you must be willing to embrace the discomfort without going backward.

If you want to stop doing something that is destroying you, you must decide to learn how to love yourself. If you've been distracting yourself all of your life, you do not even know who you are. Re-engaging in an addictive pattern might feel like the loving thing to do, but in reality, it is the hateful thing to do. Growing is critical to your success. If you do not learn how to embrace your feelings and then reroute them toward love rather than fear, you will remain trapped. Using substances, dysfunctional relationships, or any other addiction is never a loving thing to do. When you feel uncomfortable, remember to re-center and keep moving forward. Now is the time to visualize a future out of the maze.

Love versus Pain

When our caretakers failed to love us and hurt us instead, we learned to equate love with pain. *If my parents are supposed to love me, why are they treating me this way?* is the thought process of a child who has been abused or neglected. This template carries over into our future relationships, leading us to think the deeper the pain, the more that we love. As Christian told me, "I must really love Marlena; even though she's unfaithful, I can't be without her. When we fight, I can't eat, I can't sleep, I can't do anything but think about her. I just want to die until I'm back in her arms." Christian was gripped with fear, causing him to confuse love with pain. In therapy, he was able to recognize that he felt worthless as a child because his parents never seemed to want him around. Whenever Marlene rejected him and acted out by ignoring him, he relived the disheartened feelings he experienced in his youth. He was able to justify the abuse because of his childhood pain template, plus Marlene was as nurturing as she was distant. He knew pain quite well but never had the good feelings this relationship offered. When the nurturing was withdrawn, he felt unplugged from the only emotional connection he had ever experienced. Consumed with fear that he would never have the good relationship parts again, Christian's thinking blurred any sense of reality about his future.

When Christian learned how to feel good through self-respect, he was able to break the pattern with Marlene. When she would withdraw, he stopped chasing her and waited until she came back to him. He then insisted she participate in couples therapy so that they could grow together. Soon, she was willing to learn about her own pain template and developed better ways to communicate her feelings, Christian was able to hear her, and their relationship improved.

Brenda sought help because she could not understand why she was having problems with her coworkers. She said office personnel would suddenly turn on her, and she could not understand why. She appeared to be disassociating; she could not remember the event that led up to the altercation. This form of self-protection starts in childhood as a defense mechanism as self-protection from invasive emotional overload. The child's mind simply checks out and does not remember the traumatic event that precipitated the lapse. The same conditioned amnesic response follows any future perceived trauma.

As a child, Brenda was physically beaten and sexually abused. She was passed from relative to relative and there was no stability in her life. At two years sober, she met her boyfriend, James, and they moved in together. Within weeks, her childhood nightmare was reenacted. They both worked, but Brenda was responsible for the home. When James came home, he would inspect the house and criticize any imperfections he could find. Tired of being berated, Brenda started to stick up for herself, and James began screaming at her. As the emotional abuse escalated, he began striking Brenda whenever she stood up to him. The crisis was always followed by makeup sessions of remorse, gifts, and lovemaking: a classic domestic-abuse cycle.

In spite of the community resources available to her, Brenda felt trapped financially, and she said James was the only person who offered her the stability of a home. She committed to the learn, grow, and forgive process, but when James found out she was in therapy, he threatened to kick her out of the house and refused to get therapy with her. Brenda was not ready to move into a shelter for women and lose the lifestyle she was enjoying for the first time in her life. As difficult as it would be, she was going to have to make more sacrifices before she could fully recover from her lifelong trauma. She would have to dig deep within herself and look outside of herself for inspiration and assistance to heal and rebuild a life of her own. Since James was unwilling to get help, Brenda would have to remove herself so that the cycle of abuse would be stopped, and she could benefit from therapy without constant setbacks at home. She had to choose between two forms of pain: the lasting one that would keep recurring as long as she stayed, and the temporary pain that would be a part of her healing process. After referring her to a domestic-abuse shelter, I did not hear back from her.

Love is not pain, and pain is not love. The pure emotion of joy will never produce negative feelings. Love can heal pain; it never causes pain. Pain comes from loss and the fear that we will never have love again. Once we learn to separate these two emotions, we can be clear about our choice between love and fear. Even though it is painful to lose a loved one, most of the pain is sustained by the ego. The ego tells us we failed, we will never find love again, we will never recover from the loss, it is our fault, and myriad similar messages. These fear-based thoughts cause us to hold on, rather than let go. When we cannot take a leap of faith, we stay stuck, and new love is blocked from finding its way to us.

You can love someone even when you are not with them. You can love someone even when they hurt you. You can love someone who does not want to be with you. You can love someone you do not want. Love is always present within you. You are the one who must allow yourself to feel the love rather than hold on to the pain. Love may change form—from romance to friendship—but it does not go away unless you shut it out. When you allow your relationships to end without blame, you're able to learn and grow from those experiences.

Love's thought system is the opposite of the ego's thought system:

Love's Thought System: Out of the Maze

For Myself ← → **Love** → ← For You

↑↓

It's Not My Fault ← → **No Anger or Guilt** ← → It's Not Your Fault

↑↓

I'm Lovable ← → **No Fear** ← → You're Lovable

There Is Only Love

We Can Learn and Grow Together

Freedom from Pain

When we learn to choose love, we use all disappointments as opportunities to learn and grow. Without anger or guilt guiding us, we do not attack or blame ourselves or others. When our fear is exposed, it loses a grip on us. Instead, we choose love to guide us through hurt and fear. We lose tolerance for hurting and being hurt, and we learn the difference between harm and help. Even though the loving choice may sometimes feel cruel or hurtful, this is not the case when we come from love.

Jerry told me when she finally recovered from her divorce, she met Bart through work, and the chemistry they felt was a mixture of friendship and "sizzling attraction." Jerry said it was maddening to be so drawn to someone who was so alluring but who could not consummate a relationship. They would spend hours talking and flirting, but after several months, they still had not gone on a date. Even though the situation was painful for Jerry, she continued to hold on, month after month. She suspected that Bart had a secret, and rather than stepping back, the intrigue only further compelled her to help Bart move forward. Jerry worked harder and harder to make something happen, but all that she got from Bart was more words and more sizzles. During the next two years, Jerry and Bart continued their tortuous dance, and though their relationship became physical, Bart had not changed his mind-set at all. Jerry was intoxicated with the illusion that things would change, while she remained gut-hooked on a person who could not love her.

Jerry did not realize she was continually reenacting a relationship with her childhood father, from whom she could never get enough attention. She felt that he loved her, yet there was always something to compete with: work, commitments, responsibilities, siblings. She was forever in a state of longing, now reenacted with Bart. To heal, she had to channel all her energy directed toward Bart back to healing herself—her compulsion to stop competing for love. She would have to learn about her pain template with her father and grieve what she did not have with him before she could find a relationship that could offer true intimacy.

Just as we learned to distinguished irrational fear from intuitive warnings, we also need to differentiate between healthy grieving and suffering. Grief is a natural, temporary response to a loss; suffering is a refusal to let go of the loss. When we hold on to our emotions of anger, guilt, and fear, we remain in an addictive mentality, staying forever stuck in the pain maze. When we lose someone or something we love, we let go of the pain by feeling the sorrow.

These are only a few examples of how pain and love can be confused. If you are experiencing pain in your relationships, love is not the cause. When you have learned to treat yourself with kindness, you will turn your focus from hurting to loving. You will grow and share that fullness with others. The more you share, the more you will feel the love that you are.

All relationships are perfectly designed to provide opportunities to learn and grow. The true purpose of any relationship is to love and be loved. *Learn, Grow, Forgive,* offers the tools to remove the obstacles that are blocking the love. If we recognize that most pain is rooted in the past, we can heal those stored memories. When we remember to be still with our feelings, allow them to surface, and release them, they lose their hold on us. The walls of the maze will slowly crumble, removing the barriers to the love that already is within us. The world will only reflect back to you the love that you have for yourself.

You do not have to seek what you already have. The harder you look for love, the farther away it moves. The more love you share, the more love you attract. This paradox exists because love is complete and seeks only to magnify itself, never to fill a void. When people meet and share love, then is love complete, and there is no room for pain. The most important love affair you will ever have is with yourself.

Moment of Reflection: What Does Love Mean to You?

1. How would you define love?

___

___

___

2. Did you feel loved when you were young?

___

___

___

3. Do you use the level of pain you feel as a barometer for love?

___

___

___

4. List the ways you have treated yourself in a loveless manner. Keep in mind, putting up with abusive behavior from others is loveless too.

___

___

___

5. Do you recognize that if you stop looking for love and start being the love you want, love will find its way to you? How will you show love to others?

____

____

____

6. If you feel pain in your relationship, how can you replace it with love?

____

____

____

7. List the times you unconsciously chose fear over love in a relationship: What would you do differently now?

____

____

____

8. How many red hearts are now in your jar? ________________

Additional Journal Space

Part III

Forgive

11

Chapter

The Ultimate Healing

Forgiveness offers everything I want.
—*A Course in Miracles*

If you have come this far, take the time to congratulate yourself for moving out of the maze. If you do not feel prepared for this final step, keep working on learning and growing until you are ready.

If you have learned how your emotional state developed and you have grown through healing, you are ready for a genuine spiritual connection. With an open heart and mind, you are now free to love and be loved.

Spirituality and mental health are intertwined because spirituality is love. All of the chants, prayers, and meditations will never bring us to our spirit if we remain walled off by old wounds. Many people bypass the psychological healing and try to be spiritual, only to later wonder why their lives have not improved. Forgiveness is the final step to achieving spiritual success. No matter what happened, you can heal and forgive, and then those experiences can be used to help others.

Here is what our lives look like when we embrace forgiveness:

Love's Thought System: Forgiveness

For Myself ← → **Love** → ← For You

↑↓

It's Not My Fault ← → **No Anger or Guilt** ← → It's Not Your Fault

↑↓

I'm Lovable ← → **No Fear** ← → You're Lovable

There Is Only Love

We All Make Mistakes

We Forgive

We Heal Together

We Help Others to Heal

For many, forgiveness is the hardest part of the healing process: "I will never forgive him for being unfaithful to me." "I live to get even with her for embezzling money from my business." "My daughter was raped and murdered. Forgive? Are you kidding?" "I will always resent my mother for making me do that." "I'll never get over this divorce; he betrayed the children and me when he left us for another man." "I can't forget when my brother humiliated me in front of my friends." "I'll never forgive myself for that." "I don't believe in God; if there is one, he's cruel to let all of these innocent children suffer." Sound familiar? These are actual woes that patients have shared. They live by them, even when they serve no useful purpose.

People who have been violated in unimaginable ways may have difficulty forgiving, but it is of no use to them to be tied to the past. I have often heard the expression, "I can forgive, but I will not forget."

This type of thought may help someone psychologically, but it is not fully embracing the joy of spiritual healing. Forgiveness and forgetting are the same; once we forgive, we do not care to remember the grievance.

Tranquility comes from letting go of resentments: the toxic emotional waste that you may have lugged around for many years. If you focus on the past, you are not aware of what is happening right now, especially all the good things. Like elephants chained to a post they could easily pull away, if they only tried, we need only to decide to release the chains that bind us.

Maybelle was referred for depression after suffering an unimaginable tragedy. It had been three years since her daughter, Flo had been murdered. Maybelle was feeling so poorly, she could not work. She told me that her daughter had been shot while standing on the side of the street, talking to a friend. The murderer had been on the same street earlier to buy drugs, but instead, the drug dealer took his money and then yanked the gold chains off his neck and fled. Enraged, the scorned man went home, got his rife, returned, and randomly fired at everyone on the street corner. Flo's death was immeidate. The killer was caught, tried, and convicted, but he served no time. He agreed to drug treatment, and Marybelle received a cash settlement for the loss of her daughter. Money did not fix Marybelle's pain. In therapy, she allowed herself to feel her own rage and suffering, and she cried until there were no more tears. Her pain was so deep, I could feel my own heart ache for her. She wrote a letter to the murderer and told him that he took her only child, who she would never see again, and who she missed every moment of the day. She told him he had no right to Flo, but he was the one who had to live with that the rest of his life. She then told him that someday, not now, but some day, she would be able to forgive him. Marybelle continued working through her residual grief and was finally able to find a sense of peace as forgiveness slowly seeped into her dissolving pain.

Your Attack on Me Tells Me What Happened to You

People who have been abused often become abusers. They are not born that way; it is in their template. Each one of us, in some way, has been a victim of an imperfect world. If we could see the attacker with a wounded inner child, we could have compassion. If we learn to look past the wrongful act and see more deeply into what led to that behavior, we will have a greater understanding of human frailty and error. Just as our templates have led us to wander in the maze, others are caught in their own nightmares.

It's Okay to be Human

A *Course in Miracles* teaches that beneath every resentment is self-condemnation. The real reason you cannot forgive is that you blame yourself for being wronged. Patients have told me, "If I had been smarter, this would not have happened." "I'm being punished for a mistake." "I had this coming to me; bad karma." We are human, and it is impossible to live a life free from mistakes. Your greatest regrets can turn into your greatest strengths.

Can you forgive your own mistakes? Can you sit with those feelings, apologize, and let go of those awful emotions, or will you carry this burden forever? Down deep, when we are holding onto the past, we blame ourselves for those mistakes. "I should have known better," "I should have listened to my gut," "I am an idiot" are some of the labels that we assign to ourselves when we fail to make the best choices. Even small children blame themselves when others mistreat them. Without forgiveness, there will always be someone to blame.

Let Go, Let Love

Lasting resentments must be banished from your mind if you are to be free. Imagine that you are carrying a ten-pound bag of potatoes on your back, and each potato represents a resentment. You lug that sack with you wherever you go. In the morning, you drag it out of bed with you. It goes into the shower with you and sits on your back with every meal. It is with you at the movies, when you start a new relationship, and when you make love. Resentments are the drag-along burdens that accompany you everywhere. Turning resentments into forgiveness does not mean you are a victim who allows people to walk all over you. If someone is violating you, you stand up for yourself, but you do it with love, not anger.

After being betrayed, you may wonder if you will ever trust again. You can trust again once you stop blaming yourself—for not being smart enough, not knowing better, or feeling less than perfect. Trust will come when your pain is healed, and you have learned and grown from your experiences. You will trust that no matter what happened to you, you can be stronger and more loving than ever before. Your resentments can be transformed into gratitude for the lesson learned. Trust in yourself is the only trust you will ever truly need.

Ramon, a security guard, approached me after *A Course in Miracles* class one night. He was helping me pack up supplies and asked me about the textbook. Ready to end a day of seeing patients and teaching, part of me wanted to give him a rapid response and walk away. I shifted my perception when I looked into his kindly brown eyes and saw his sincere curiosity. I was reminded of the *Course's* message that "every encounter is a holy encounter" and knew that I needed to answer his earnest inquiry. I briefly explained that it was a course that teaches how to choose love over fear and that our happiness depends on being able to forgive. Then, with an animated response and light-filled eyes, he humbled me with his profound words of wisdom: "Oh, I understand that. When I was a lot younger, I met a girl and fell in love. I don't think she ever loved me, and it took a long time for me to realize that she just wanted things from me. It didn't work out, but I know that she didn't mean to hurt me. I was sad for a long time, but I knew I would be okay. After that, I kept meeting women who were the same way, but each time I learned a little bit more, and somehow, I knew inside that there was a reason for the pain and that I was changing and becoming smarter. Finally, I met my wife. She was more like me. We enjoy giving to each other. Now we've been happily married for over twenty-four years, and I'm glad for all of those experiences."

Speechless, as I listened to Ramon share his life, I was blown away with his natural ability to utilize the same principles that I had worked for years to achieve. He used his uncomfortable life experiences to learn, grow, and forgive without any formal education or training. If Ramon had not had those disappointments, he would not have the same appreciation for his wife. He was an example of someone who had the type of childhood that allowed him to stay connected to his inner spiritual guidance. He was able to go with the flow of whatever life handed him, without blame or suffering. Ramon understood that if he kept an open heart, he would find true love. When he was hurt, he could have closed his heart and missed the blessings that were to come. Rather than becoming cynical and self-protective after his first and deepest heartbreak, he allowed himself to heal, he moved forward, and then he tried again and again until he met the person who was just right for him.

You Are More Innocent Than You Think

The *Course in Miracles* tells us that there is no sin, only errors, and that if we correct those mistakes, we will be free. This does not mean that we do not have a role in our unfortunate circumstances or that we are faultless. I have seen many people who could not understand their role in their problems, and the problems stayed with them. Once a person takes responsibility for how they have co-created a situation and corrects it, the problem can then go away. Sometimes, simply acknowledging the mistake will provide all of the amends necessary. When we have the courage to face our dark side so that we can learn and grow, we can become as healthy as we want to be. Like pulling the weeds out of the garden, we remove the old guilt trips that strangle the possibility of new growth. If you permit yourself to be human, you will be able to gather the lessons from those mistakes rather than suffer a lifelong sentence. The most important person you will ever forgive is yourself.

A final consideration before going on: What if, before you were even born, you were the one who planned your life script? You decided all of the fun things you wanted to experience as well as the challenging lessons you wanted to learn here on earth. What if some of those experiences meant a great deal of betrayal and pain so that you could learn the highest act of forgiveness and compassion? What if you had purposely chosen your parents, your siblings, your career, successes, and failures—all for the benefit of your spiritual growth? If this were true, is it possible this perfect curriculum was designed to help you to fulfill your life's purpose?

A *Course in Miracles* teaches us that a miracle is merely a change in perception. Are you willing to perceive your past differently and consider the possibility that you designed it for a higher purpose? Are you ready to have the miracle? Now is the time to fulfill your life's purpose.

Moment of Reflection: Forgiveness Exercises

1. Make a list of everyone you have not forgiven, and describe what happened. Identify how you might be blaming yourself for those situations.

___

___

___

2. For what have you not forgiven yourself? Make a list.

3. What happened in your life that led to those mistakes? What did you learn?

5. How have you grown when you were hurt? Have you remained stuck in fear? How?

6. Do you think you receive any benefit from keeping resentments? What might happen if you let go of them?

7. If you could write your future life script, what would it look like?

A Way to Forgiveness

1. Wait until you feel 100 percent ready.
2. Once you feel certain that the time is right, make sure you have at least a couple of hours, so that you can complete and fully benefit from the exercise.
3. First, identify a person you want to forgive, even if deceased.
4. Write that person a letter, reciting everything you remember and how hurt you felt.
5. Referring to the letter, look for any area that you felt at fault.
6. Read the letter out loud, go slowly, and meditate, allowing all of your feelings to surface.
7. Tell the person you forgive him or her. Then tell yourself you are forgiven.

Practice this exercise with every person or situation that comes up, but only once for each. If something new surfaces, repeat the exercise. It is important that after you do this exercise, you refrain from dwelling on the resentment or guilt that you've released. If it does reenter your mind, say, "We are forgiven." Once you have forgiven, there is no reason to relive the situation.

Additional Journal Space

12

Chapter

Honoring Truth: The Doorway to Authenticity

Rather fail with honor than succeed by fraud.
—Sophocles

When we have forgiven ourselves and the world, we no longer live in guilt and fear. Living in fear causes us to hold on to unhealthy attachments and dependencies. Free from the past, and forgiving all that has happened, we desire the type of love that honors freedom with trust. Many of us go through a great deal of learning, growing, and forgiving before we finally exit the maze, and that's okay. Once we are out of the trap, we no longer imprison ourselves or others. Forgiveness, the final part of the healing process, allows us to walk the pathway to relationships that offer genuine love.

Now that you are out of the maze (or at least know how to get out), you can recognize that the dysfunctional guides of anger, guilt, and fear only bring pain; you are now free to be your true self in the present. Those of us raised in dysfunctional families learned to hide our real feelings and bury them deep inside. Children who are encouraged to speak up for what they want and how they feel learn to reveal an authentic self to the world. If you are not true to yourself, it is impossible to be happy with someone else. The real you is the most appealing you.

Many relationships suffer because we are not honest with ourselves or others. We pretend we are expressing our wants and needs, but we do not risk exposing our true feelings for fear of losing the relationship or fear of being indebted. It is better to grow through the fear and show your true thoughts and feelings than hiding behind the mask of an imposter. How many times have you been in a group, and people did not speak up and say what they wanted to do? Have you felt frustrated with the way someone was treating you and stuffed your feelings rather than say something? Has it been difficult for you to ask for your monetary value in work or business? Have other people been running your life, and it seems you have no control over your destiny? Have you been accused of things that you did not do but were unable to defend yourself? Have you stopped yourself from speaking up because you thought things would magically improve on their own?

We act in these ways because we fear rejection, but when you hide who you are, you reject yourself. If fear has silenced you, you now can choose to align with the truth that will set you free. The final part of growing is to go beyond that lost part of yourself and speak your truth. When you communicate your true feelings with love, you have succeeded at honoring yourself and the relationship. If you are not true to yourself, you cannot expect anyone else to honor you.

Find the Words

When fear blocks honesty, silence can be justified in many ways. We might say it is better to take the high road, silence is golden, or we must avoid conflict at all cost. It is not difficult for people to discuss their disagreements calmly. Rather than psyching ourselves out of conflict resolution, we can courageously embrace our differences and address them.

Authentic communication is the doorway out of fear toward healthy, bonded relationships. All relationships will bring up old behaviors that you can now replace in new and loving ways. Healthy relationships recognize that we might step on one another's toes, and these situations need to be discussed. If someone does not care if you are hurting, you do not matter much to that person. You cannot lose a friend you never had. The notion that "I am not responsible for your feelings" is a doorway to disaster. Problem-solving is the fundamental basis of any lasting connection. Relationships are a we program, not a me program.

Be the Solution, Not the Confusion

Sometimes, out of fear, we communicate in a sideways manner, causing the other person to feel confused or manipulated. It is wiser to be straightforward than to play a word game of hide-and-seek. Taking the risk of saying something wrong is better than pretending. You can always apologize for an incorrect comment, but your truth cannot be honored in silence.

Bobby had been stuffing his feelings most of his life and yet learned how to be honest with his wife. Resentful over paying bills they could not afford and being thousands of dollars in debt, he was afraid to address the matter with his wife. In therapy, he remembered that as a child, he was shamed and made to feel selfish when asking for what he wanted. These memories made him realize he was still functioning as a small, helpless child. With this awareness, he was able to choose love over fear. He spoke with his wife about their debt and proposed they work on a budget. At first, his wife was defensive, but when he told her he loved her and wanted to have less financial stress on his shoulders, she became supportive and kept to a budget. Consequently, their relationship grew closer rather than further apart.

The next time you have to decide to reveal your authentic self, be aware of whether you are holding back or not. If you are, identify your fears and write them down. Once you do this, you can decide to listen to the voice of your fear-based ego or the voice of love. You are the only one who can speak your truth.

Name It, Don't Blame It

When emotionally charged, follow the previously outlined re-centering steps before expressing yourself. Remember to close your eyes, allow your feelings and memories to surface, breathe, and wait until your feelings neutralize. Once you are calm, you are free to communicate with love. At this point, you might feel it is not necessary to say anything. You realize that your anger was about the past. However, be careful; the ego has a tricky way of keeping us in the maze. Even if it was about the past, you still stay focused on the current issue. For example: "Yesterday when you were late, I did not mention it, but I was upset. I realize this had nothing to do with you. When I thought about it, I remembered all the times my mother kept me waiting in the empty parking lot at school. I feel anxious when people are late." This type of communication is honest and vulnerable while letting the other person know why you reacted. When you do not blame, you have created the space for the other person to become better attuned to you without being defensive.

Facts and Feelings

Authentic communication means being straight and honest about your deepest desires. You communicate with love and logic. Be conscious that what you are saying is factual and true, not distorted and fictional. It is easy to be open and vulnerable when you are not angry, guilty, or fearful. Focus only the present situation and not the past. Comments like "You always ..." or "You never ..." must be banned from loving communication. Equally as important, you listen to what others have to say, while you earnestly try to understand their message.

Effective and loving communication means expressing facts and making specific requests. For example, "Yesterday when you left without saying goodbye, I felt sad. Would you give me a hug or kiss before you leave?" This statement has no judgment, is fact-based, and is a specific request. The communicator is emotionally vulnerable without expressing anger or guilt. There is no guarantee that the other person will hear you or even care how you feel, but you have stated what you truly want. Here are some other examples of expressing honesty without judgment: "I'm sorry that you failed your test/got a DUI/missed work again. I love you, and it is painful to see you hurt. I want to support you, but I won't be able to fix this for you. I believe that you will learn and grow from this experience." In all of these examples, the communicator does not express anger, fear, or guilt but speaks with kindness and dignity. The goal is to bring someone closer, not blow them away.

Sharon and Donald met at a party and started dating right away. They were married a year later and within two years had their first child, Aaron. Sharon loved being a mother, but shortly after Aaron's birth, she and Donald drifted apart. Donald started working long hours; he went out for drinks with coworkers at the end of his day and spent very little time at home on the weekends. When Sharon was bored and lonely, she shopped online to fill her sense of emptiness. Neither Donald nor Sharon were able to communicate feelings about the changes in their marriage, and their moments of intimacy were increasingly infrequent.

When they came in for counseling, they were contemplating divorce. Donald admitted he was angry and said that he had felt neglected ever since their son was born. He also acknowledged that he felt guilty about spending so much time away from home. When asked about his fear under the anger and guilt, Donald thought that Sharon did not love him and that she was only in the relationship for financial security. She acknowledged her fear that Donald might not love her either; his absences were the proof her ego needed to believe he was seeing someone else. The two of them failed to realize that templates of their parents' marriages stood between them, making them afraid of love and commitment. Once they honestly faced the walls of anger and guilt between them, they were able to get past the fear and face the reality of their situation. If they wanted to have a marriage, they would have to hear each other and spend loving time together as a couple as well as a family. When they decided to recommit to their relationship, Donald said he needed quality time alone with his wife and that he wanted to be acknowledged as a provider and a parent. He also wanted to spend more one-on-one time with his son so that he could develop a better bond with him. Sharon was delighted with his requests because they brought the family closer.

Sharon and Donald's story provides an example of how couples unconsciously fall into the same patterns they witnessed in their childhoods. Fortunately, this couple had the fearlessness to look at themselves and realize they had taken on the same roles as their parents. When Donald said he wanted quality time with Sharon to talk, feel close, and make love, their relationship grew, and unhealthy outside interests lost their appeal to both of them.

Skip the Story; Keep It Simple

When speaking your truth, the best statements are clear enough that any five-year-old can understand. Dredging up the past and telling a long story taxes the listener and triggers a reaction in the person with whom you are trying to heal. If Donald had told Sharon all of the family drama he had endured as a child, she might feel that she was paying for his parents' mistakes. However, Donald's communication was clear and simple: "I feel like I'm reliving my parents' mistakes; my dad was never home, and my mom's only interests were the kids and material things. I want us to have a better marriage. I'd like to spend at least two nights a week alone, time together as a family on the weekends, and have some one-on-one time with Aaron. Can you tell me how you feel about this? What you would like as well?"

This type of communication engages the listener and makes positive, specific requests. Most important, kind words validate rather than alienate the person you are addressing. Once trust is built, through a series of positive interactions, there is a bridge that promotes closeness rather than separateness.

When you are authentic, you create genuine connections with those you love. No one can know your true self by trying to read your mind. You may not always get what you want, but you can always be true to yourself. If you want real intimacy, the risk of revealing your true self will be well worth your effort. You no longer have to follow a script assigned to you. The real you is the best you.

The exercises below will help you to identify how you might have blocked yourself from being seen and heard by those you love. Upon completion, be sure to put some more red hearts in your jar.

Moment of Reflection: Honoring Your Truth

1. Do you feel that the people you are closest to know the real you?

___

___

___

2. Do you equate differences with others as conflict?

___

___

___

3. Do you withhold affection or communication when you feel hurt rather than lovingly communicate what hurt you?

____

____

____

4. Do you appease people because you feel guilty or fearful?

____

____

____

5. Do you communicate when you are angry, or do you wait until your feelings are neutralized?

____

____

____

6. Are you willing to show your true feelings? Based on what you have learned, how will you do this?

____

____

____

Additional Journal Space

13

Chapter

An Open Heart: The Strongest Heart

The best and most beautiful things in the world cannot be seen or even touched. They must be felt with the heart.
—Helen Keller

When I was a hurting little girl, I asked for help, and a spiritual sense of comfort came to me. Not sure what this connection was, I named it God, and I did find solace. As time went on, so did the trauma, and by the time I was a teenager, I was too deeply troubled to seek this comforting presence. Instead, alcohol and cigarettes were my replacements for the genuine spiritual comfort I had received as a child. Thankfully, in spite of the death wish I had, that presence never left me. It was reawakened in my early twenties when I first read the *Desiderata*, instilling me with inspiration to reconnect with that earlier source of love. Though it has been a lifelong process, this was the point in time when my heart reopened, and my spiritual recovery began.

A hardened heart cannot embrace the emotional spectrum of being fully alive. When my heart was closed, I lived in a world of black and white, with no appreciation for the beauty all around me. I did not see my precious daughter, her smiling face, her sad eyes. I did not see the beautiful area in which I lived, with its gorgeous waterways, swaying palm trees, and historic architecture. I did not see the comfortable home I was blessed to live in or appreciate the nice car or the person who gave it to me. I did not look at the faces that passed me by; they were just more of the background scenery to which I was indifferent. I did not taste the delicious food on my plate or feel the cool breeze on my skin. My closed mind and an unfeeling heart took me from one blurry event to the next, one minute to the next, with no appreciation for the gift of life and all that it was offering me.

After years of healing, the calcification around my heart began to dissolve. A small ray of love entered, leaving me wide open, and nothing was ever the same. Suddenly, I saw the beauty, tasted the deliciousness of life, and felt my surroundings. My senses transformed from black and white into living color. The more my heart opened, the more love came to me. I now am filled with so much love that almost every moment is exhilarating.

The Heart Needs No Protection

Sometimes, it is difficult to forgive because we are afraid of being hurt again. Using our resentments as armor, we feel a false sense of security that we think will protect us from future disappointments. It is only natural that when we are deeply hurt, we close our hearts. The more wounded we are, the tighter our heart closes. A closed heart is not protection; instead, it's a burden to carry and can lead to depression, hopelessness, and even a heart attack. An unforgiving heart is too wounded and closed for love to enter.

If we protect ourselves from pain, we also shield ourselves from all joyful emotions. We cannot have it both ways. We either learn to keep our heart open and grow with everything that life gives us, or it becomes like an impenetrable rock. A forgiving heart is healed and open to receive all that love offers.

Brett told me that by the time he was five, he was obsessed with "getting off of the planet." He did not remember having anyone to do things with and was frequently alone for hours and hours. His parents were working most of the time and left him with his abusive and neglectful grandmother. She locked him in a bedroom whenever she wanted to sleep, watch her favorite television shows, or have someone over. He told me he was so miserable and frustrated, he would bang his head against the wall. He never knew what time his parents would pick him up, if at all. When he was with them, they had no patience, and he was either being yelled at or completely ignored. He said he didn't have a clue how to stick up for himself, and he often felt used by his friends. On one occasion, an older teenager seduced him. He was baffled by his willingness to agree to this simply for the pleasure that the attention brought him. Consumed with confusion and shame, he decided to avoid people at all costs and became a loner.

He concluded that relationships were too painful and that he was never going to feel again. It was not until now, at age thirty, after his first girlfriend broke up with him, that all his pent-up pain gushed forth. "At first," he said, "like always, I did not care, but then I began to notice I could not get comfortable in my own skin. It has been getting worse every day. I feel like I'm five years old again, and I don't want to be here anymore."

Fortunately, Brett wanted out of his pain maze and sought therapy. He was willing to learn and grow so that he could be released from his emotional prison. As he began to open up and to cry, he was able to receive the comfort that therapy offered, and he felt relief each time he released his sorrow. As he healed, his heart opened up and welcomed the feelings he formerly fought. He was then able to externalize the trauma rather than continuing to blame himself. Over time, Brett was willing to forgive his parents, grandmother, and perpetrator while reclaiming his childhood innocence.

Love Is the Way

There are many reasons that your heart closes; it can be a conscious decision or something that happens over time, through self-medicating with addictions. Discovering your heart for the first time can be a beautiful experience, or it can be threatening. Once your heart opens, and love flows in, there is no turning back.

Mary emotionally checked out because she "could not tolerate the pain." Her father was abusive, and her mother could see no wrong in him. Mary endured beatings and insults until she "left her body and disappeared" and she continued to disassociate herself from any perceived discomfort or trauma. She went through life compliant and mechanical but aware something was missing. Whenever her feelings would to surface, she drank wine or took Xanax. When she became pregnant and could not medicate her feelings, she felt crazy and sought therapy.

After Mary gave birth to her first child, everything changed. She felt love for the first time in her life. "When I looked at her, a never-before feeling rushed through me. My warm tears of joy drenched her little warm body, as I held her in my arms. I clearly remember thinking, *This is what love feels like. How could anyone hurt a little child?*" Now that the door was open to Mary's emotions, she had to learn how to embrace all of the feelings: positive and negative.

Mary was fortunate that with the birth of her daughter, she found love. For the first time, she was able to embrace an emotion she had been missing all of her life. Once that light penetrated her barriers, she yearned for more. When she felt love for her child, she felt it for herself. Love motivated her to remove anything that stood in the way of being a good mother. She learned how to be with her feelings and allowed them to flow through her without acting on them. She began to trust her healing process. Over time, she was free from her painful past and able to embrace the joy of her new life.

You Are Your Best Protector

It is possible to keep an open heart and still protect yourself in healthy ways. An open heart allows feelings to move through it, holding the positive and purifying the rest. You don't accomplish this by leaving yourself wide open to situations that are not safe. When an unruly heart governs you, you are disconnected from your intuition, and you remain emotionally unstable and unhappy.

Many of my patients thought that painful things happened to them because God was punishing them. Often, bad things happen because of our own willfulness and self-interests. When we listen to our loving internal navigation system rather than the fear-based ego, we can avoid most of life's misfortunes. We learn to pay attention to what people do with our hearts, and without fear, we remain in reality. We do not make excuses for unacceptable behavior; rather, we face it. When people fall short of our expectations, we do not reject them. Instead, we use the learn, grow, and forgive process, and then we address all conflicts from a place of love. If someone is unable or unwilling to engage in healthy communication and problem-solving, we are free to let go with love. It is not necessary to stay connected to people who do not treat you well. You are the one who teaches other people how to treat you.

Stacey was a sexual-abuse survivor who had a history of giving herself to men who did not truly care for her. She told me she was confused because she felt it was wrong but enjoyed the sexual power she felt over men. She lost that control once she had sex, and the men showed a lack of commitment or consistency. She ignored those signals and allowed herself to believe a relationship existed when there was none. She came to therapy to stop the pattern. Through learning about her sexual-abuse template, she realized she was unconsciously primed to be used by men, a substitute for genuine love. She grew when she grieved the pain of the betrayal by her father and was willing to learn how to get to know a man before she slept with him. She consciously observed what men did rather than what they said. If the man's actions did not match his words, she was no longer willing to put her heart on the line for someone who would not treasure her. She learned that she deserved to be with someone who valued her, not someone who would gamble with her emotions. If we are reckless with our hearts, we are treating ourselves in a loveless manner. Recklessness comes from need, not love.

Jack had a history of being exploited by his employers. Though he had a master's degree and was a good worker, he was not earning what he was worth. He came to see me after years of resentments toward people who agreed to pay him a certain amount but then later reneged. During therapy, a clear pattern emerged: Jack had no problem with verbally negotiating but never insisted on a written contract, even though he knew he should. When it was time for a promised bonus, his employer tried to change the terms of their agreement or would avoid the topic altogether. Jack did not have a contract to fall back on, so he either had to tolerate less pay or quit his job. In therapy, Jack learned that his template formed when his father agreed to pay him an allowance for specific duties but rarely followed through, leaving Jack sad and disillusioned. He eventually stopped caring about whether his father paid him or not.

This conflict had carried over into his adult life, and if he were to break the pattern, he would have to grow. Once this unconscious drive was exposed, Jack was able to calmly address the matter with his boss. When nothing changed, he decided to look for another job. When the right opportunity presented itself, he listened to his inner guidance, ignored his anxiety, and once the employment terms were clearly written in a contract, he accepted the position. A year later, Jack achieved his financial goals, and with it came his new self-esteem.

We are strongest when we keep our hearts open. We trust the guidance of our intuition when it tells us what is safe and what is not. When life crises inevitably occur, we allow ourselves to feel the sharp arrows that strike our hearts and then feel those arrows passing right on through. There will be bleeding, but like all wounds, there also will be healing. The scar that forms around a wound is much stronger than the surrounding skin. The bigger the injury, the more it hurts, but also the greater the mend. Soon, we no longer are afraid of being hurt because we have learned that something better always waits on the other side of the pain. With each disheartening experience, we know that our hearts will grow even stronger, with an ever-expanding capacity to love.

Your heart is much stronger than you could ever imagine. It will do what you tell it to do. It is the place where all hurt can be purified and forgiven, if that is your choice. Are you willing to open your heart, release your pain, and let love enter?

How full is your jar of hearts now?

Moment of Reflection: Opening the Heart

1. Is your heart closed? If so, is it partly or completely? When did this happen? How has this benefited you? How has it hurt you?

___

___

___

2. Have you allowed your heart to feel pain?

___

___

___

3. Are you willing to see your heart as the strength that can purify all of your pain?

___

___

___

4. Are you willing to allow your heart to be open and forgive?

____

____

____

Meditation (Repeat Whenever Your Feelings Are Trying to Surface)

Close your eyes and place your focus on your heart—the place where you experience all of your feelings. Think back to some of the times that your heart was contracted or burdened with heaviness. Allow yourself to re-experience those feelings now. Imagine that each memory enters your heart, and watch as each old memory heals with every beat of your heart. Breathe through all of the emotions. Stay with this process as long as you can, knowing that your heart will only grow stronger each time it's allowed to feel a wound. Like any muscle, it gets stronger with each workout. The more your heart heals, the more it will be able to hold so much love that it will flow through every part of your being. Allow yourself to breathe in unison with the waves of emotion that you feel, like the waves on a beach. Keep allowing your heart to expand, knowing that you can trust the healing it offers and also that you can trust yourself to take care of your heart.

Additional Journal Space

14

Chapter

Higher Power, Where Are You?

The greatest act of faith takes place when a
man finally decides he is not God.
—Johann Wolfgang von Goethe

Even though you have done the work and feel free, you may at times feel abandoned and alone. When your need is the greatest, it might seem there is no one or nothing to console you. There may be several reasons for this. Perhaps you are rejecting something you do not understand, or you may be too discouraged to recognize the help that is there for you. Other times, you may be expecting an immediate solution when you simply need to sit in solitude.

I Don't See You

Some people who lack a spiritual connection are agnostic and do not believe in a creator or supreme being. Many of these people rejected a force-fed religion that did not make sense. They felt brainwashed and did not believe they were sinners destined for hell. When people are coerced into thinking a certain way, there is a tendency to be closed-minded to the possibility of any higher power at all. You are free to make your own decisions about a higher power.

Some individuals only believe in what they can see. At the root of this thinking is the fear of being naive or stupid. It is irrational and illogical to believe you have to see something for it to exist. No one could see a cure for bacterial infections, yet penicillin only needed to be discovered. No one could see other galaxies, yet they existed long before the invention of high-powered telescopes. No one can see an early pregnancy, yet a small life is forming before it is ever visible.

Some agnostics who have been healed by learning, growing, and forgiving become more open to spirituality. I asked them, "If there were a God, how would you describe him?" and they can articulate a clear vision. One patient thought it was an invisible force that worked through all of nature. Another woman told me that there was a *Matrix*-type system that kept everything together. Someone else said it was his conscience, the part of him that tells him right from wrong. When he listens, things turn out well; when he does not, things go poorly.

It seems that many agnostics are not always unbelievers; instead, they are rejecting religious beliefs that did not make sense to them. Once free to develop a personal sense of divinity, they often find a belief system that does fit for them. Willingness to open your mind to the possibility of a God or master creator—and allow yourself to receive that personalized concept—is all that is ever required. *A Course in Miracles* teaches that each one of us has a holy spirit, part of the divine spirit, and we only need to learn how to access this source. If you do not understand the concept of spirit, you need only to understand love because that is all that ever really matters.

You Don't Hear Me

Sometimes, people feel their higher power is ignoring them. Patients have told me there have been times they have not felt comforted in moments of desperation. They pray and pray but do not feel better. *A Course in Miracles* teaches that God is with us wherever we are because a part of God is within every one of us. If God is in all of us, how is it possible that there is no help when we need it the most?

When asking for help, you might think you are listening to your own thoughts, and you disregard the message altogether. It is very important when you pray for guidance, you are willing to accept the loving messages you receive. Once, when I was railing at God to explain the overwhelming pain in my life, I heard a clear message in my mind that said, *Donna, all of your problems, all of your life, are related to alcohol.* Though I was shocked, it was a moment of clarity and truth that set me on an entirely new path. It was true: Alcoholism racked my childhood with pain, it ruined my marriage, and it now had a hold on me. My ego told me the answer was not that simple, and if I had listened to my ego, I would not be writing this book. Your answers might show up in a multitude of ways: dreams, reappearing messages wherever you look, the same suggestions from different sources, or a powerful sense of the right action to take. All of these could be arrows pointing you in the right direction.

Sometimes, the mind is too ramped up and overloaded to receive comfort. Severe trauma can cause someone to feel a lack of relief because the mind is overloaded. In these situations, it is best to release your passions (in healthy ways that we discussed earlier), and then do your re-centering exercises and wait until your mind is calm enough to receive the clarity you seek. It is also essential to reach out to loved ones who can help you.

During your spiritual journey, there may have been times when the pain has brought you to your knees. I have worked with patients who have experienced the unimaginable, losing their children to addiction, incurable illnesses, and even murder. Even this inconsolable suffering can heal when adequately mourned. Deep pain has deep roots and needs to be released. It is only natural that when the pain is too intense, we want to move as far away from it as possible. Avoiding the ache does not make it go away; it just slips into the invisible baggage that we unconsciously drag around. We need to honor our pain as part of a necessary grieving process, lest our grief is buried alive. Once the pain subsides, we can begin to look at how we might have done things differently had we been more connected to that inner guiding voice. Sometimes, we expect a quick fix and cannot understand that there is genuine gold at the root of our pain. Spiritual maturity means we stay with our feelings and wait for the right answers to come. Those feelings motivate us to keep learning, growing, and forgiving, even after we think we are fixed. Your spiritual growth is always a work in progress. You are never alone.

All I Need Is God

An additional barrier to feeling a higher power's presence is the exclusion of people. When we are not open to loving relationships, we are operating from fear and an unforgiven past. We must be willing to get over old pain, grieve lost connections, and let in new love. If we have not loved people, we have not found that divine source. God is love, and love manifests itself through people. Isolation and emotional walls keep out those who are here to help us through tough times. If we deliberately turn our backs on the remedy, we will not be forced to accept emotional support. If we insist on independence, our higher power will not step over those who are ready and able to comfort us.

Joanna was one of those patients who had inconsolable pain. Her ten-year marriage ended when her husband left her and their two children for her best friend. The blow left Joanna so debilitated that she could not get out of bed. After two weeks, her desperate mother called me to request a home visit. When I met Joanna, she was extremely thin, had completely neglected any personal care, and would do nothing except read the Bible. She told me that she did not want to talk about anything and that only God could help her. She had been praying day and night for weeks, but she just felt worse. She said she would kill herself if she didn't have children.

Joanna's prolonged recovery from her trauma was due to her resisting help every step of the way. She expected God to lift her out of despair. It was easier to put the responsibility for her life on something other than herself. Her fantasy of being rescued by God would never happen because we are given tears to release our pain and grow. We also are given one another to support us through those unbearable times. When emotionally harmful things happen, we tend to close off from those around us. No one can find their way to success in the pitch-black.

After I visited with Joanna several times, she finally began to express her anger, and after a couple of weeks, the tears started to flow. She admitted she did not want to cry because she might not be able to stop. She learned that by giving in to her sorrow, she was gaining strength. Once she started opening up in therapy, she was able to share her pain with others and did not have to carry her emotional burden all alone. At this point, she realized that she had placed all of her emotional eggs in one basket: her husband. Her prolonged recovery from her trauma was due to her resistance every step of the way. Once she let other people in, she realized people did want to love her and be in her life.

Real growth and forgiveness occurred when Joanna was able to tell me that she understood why her husband left her. In her words, she had become "a passive, self-absorbed housewife, bored, who only performed duties for her house and children." She had lost any desire to have a life of her own outside of the marriage, and she admitted that she ignored her husband's subtle comments about feeling the marriage was in a rut. She realized that she was constantly finding fault with him and rarely appreciated his efforts. It took courage for her to face this truth, but by doing so, she discovered the key to forgiveness, which freed her from being a victim.

Who's in Charge?

Spiritual relief eludes us when we take charge and push God into the passenger seat. We find it difficult to trust in an unseen God who allows terrible things to happen. When hurtful things happen to you, it feels unnatural to have faith that situations will be handled without your involvement. Until you let go and allow life to evolve, you will find it challenging to develop trust in a divine order. Some catastrophes are never understood, but if you want to heal fully, you must be willing to forgive. If you do not trust, you have not forgiven.

A *Course in Miracles* tells us that seeing the world as meaningless creates fear and causes us to place ourselves in competition with God, thinking we can do a better job. If you are trying to manage things beyond your control, keep doing the forgiveness exercises until you can let go. By healing each new wave of pain through learning, growing, and forgiving, you can begin to make sense of the nonsensical. Releasing the pain will help you to reach a deeper understanding of the crisis that befell you. No matter how deep your wound, you can recover and move forward into a life of new meaning. You need only look at all the miracles that have arisen from disasters to know this is true. Even amidst the horror of 9/11, people came together and adversaries united; some found a new cause, and helping others replaced self-centeredness. Love sprang forth all over the country.

It is impossible to know everything or to see the whole picture of life. An essential aspect of spiritual maturity is learning to go with the flow. We always have free will. If we start forcing things to happen, it is as if the universe steps back and says, "All right, see if your way works better than the divine plan." It's like hiring an architect to `l`create a set of plans for a house, yet you tell the builder to disregard the plans by changing doorways, window placements, and roof lines. The result is a chaotic structural mess rather than a beautifully designed home that you can enjoy.

When we learn to be patient and allow things to unfold in their own way and their own time, our own expectations are exceeded. Our part is to work on ourselves and then sit in the passenger seat and trust the process. We will never run out of work to do on ourselves. By reining control inward rather than outward, we allow success to find its way to us.

Sherry decided she wanted to start a whole new life after her divorce. She stopped drinking, started therapy, and pursued a spiritual quest. She went back to school and earned her stockbroker's license. So far, so good; she did the footwork, and now it was time to pursue her career. She went online and submitted applications to numerous firms. She had a couple of leads and made the necessary calls. As each day went by, she became more and more anxious. Rather than trusting the process and keeping busy with other temporary work, she wrote numerous letters and made several calls to companies where she had applied. This was not so bad, but after two or three calls to the same firm, she turned herself into a liability rather than an asset.

When we discussed waiting to see what would happen, Sherry felt I did not understand how desperate she was. She blamed God for things not happening fast enough and the employers for being "unprofessional" by keeping her waiting. She did not realize that time was her friend, not her enemy. She was missing an opportunity to develop spiritual maturity. After much suffering, she agreed to use the time to do the learn, grow, and forgive work, and through her efforts, she realized that waiting was a core issue for her. She remembered all the times she waited for her parents. She waited for her father to get sober enough to take her to a friend's house; she waited for her mother to fix meals. This recent waiting had triggered her unhealed template, and she was able to feel her unresolved childhood emotions now reactivated. Once she grew by grieving those memories and forgiving her parents, she no longer felt the pressure to make things happen. She could use the wait time to continue to learn, grow, and forgive whenever she had the urge to make something happen. She received an unexpected check for her birthday, and then her former husband called to tell her he had a stockbroker friend who was interested in interviewing her. She felt empowered when she worked on herself rather than trying to make other people fit into her time frame. From that point on, whenever she was tempted to force something to happen, she redirected her energy back to herself, with an ever-increasing strength and sense of trust in her life.

More than anything, Justin wanted to get married and start a family. He was forty years old, successful, and ready to settle down. He had been on a spiritual path for several years. He had gone to an ashram in India and immersed himself in daily meditation and yoga.

He started therapy because he wanted to be able to commit, but all of his relationships had ended. He was rushing from one relationship to the next, without any time in between to learn, grow, and forgive so that he could better understand why his relationships were impermanent. Justin's pattern was easy to identify, but whenever I asked him about his childhood, he would say he could not remember much.

Justin was running from a ghost he did not want to face. He agreed to stop dating while in treatment and to use that time to heal. As his therapy progressed, he could see that his old template was operating like a broken record. He was able to discuss his most significant relationships and grieve those losses, but that was just the cover-up for his real pain. He could not remember why, but he did recall that he and his siblings were left unsupervised and expected to fend for themselves. They dressed, fed, and cared for themselves. There was a part of his story that was neatly tucked away in his unconscious and difficult to face. After several months, he told me the kids not only slept together but had sex with one another as well.

When Justin's hidden horrors emerged in therapy, he spent months processing the pain he had experienced as a little boy. He realized that he was terrified to get married and have a family because marriage represented the "worst pain imaginable; what if the same thing happens to my kids?" He told me he did not know how he could work, watch the children, and make sure everyone was all right; his unconscious anxiety blocked his ability to commit.

Once Justin's fear and shame were exposed, and he was able to mourn his repressed grief, his consciousness was restored to the present rather than being locked in the past. He had felt ashamed of his childhood actions, and now he could hold his parents responsible for the lack of supervision that subjected their children to harm. He was able to embrace the fact that they were children with natural impulses, without parental boundaries. He began to understand that he did not need to repeat his parents' mistakes. He had broken the pattern. Through his healing, he was no longer at the mercy of his earlier trauma. His recovery provided the self-assurance that he would not let his children suffer as he had, no matter what. Toward the end of his second year of therapy, while at a conference, he met his future wife.

Justin was successful because he was willing to learn, grow, and forgive, as success found its way into his life. If you follow the steps in the previous chapters, you too will be able to find a new sense of faith and trust.

We are told that God will never give us more than we can handle. If we believe this, then the problem is not with God, but with a lack of understanding that a higher power is always with us. If you cannot use the word *God*, then replace it with *love*. Love is always available through sharing and receiving from endless sources such as art, beauty, music, nature, children, family, and friends. When your mind is open to a higher source of communication, and your heart is open to love, your wounds will be transformed into wisdom and strength.

The exercises below can help you to address any unfinished business so that your heart is open to the love of people and a loving higher power.

Moment of Reflection: Spiritual Sustenance in Times of Need

1. What template do you have about God? What do you believe, and what do you reject? Are you willing to find your own higher power? What would that look like?

____

____

____

2. List all of the things you have neither forgiven nor forgotten in your life. Identify a time when you were hurting so badly, you felt inconsolable.

____

____

____

3. How did you handle your pain? Did you medicate it, or did you embrace it?

____

____

____

4. When you were suffering, did you keep people out? Why? Are you willing to receive help?

____

____

____

5. Are you willing to be spiritually open-minded? If so, how would you describe the God of your own understanding?

____

____

____

6. When you pray for help, are you willing to listen and trust the answers?

7. Can you look at your painful experiences as an opportunity for spiritual maturity? Describe how that has happened for you. If it has not happened for you, what possibilities do you see?

8. Are you willing to convert wait time to learn, grow, and forgive time? Do you accept that this is a lifelong process? Are you willing to do your part, go with the flow, and let outcomes find you?

9. Do you recognize that forgiveness is the doorway to spiritual sustenance in times of need? How would this appear to you?

Additional Journal Space

Chapter 15

Spiritual Success

From my own experience, I want to say that you
should follow your heart, and the mind will follow you.
Believe in yourself, and you will create miracles.
—Kailash Satyarthi

We all were born perfect—a spiritual success from the beginning. Then life happened, and our environment taught us that our imperfections made us unlovable. The, *Learn, Grow, Forgive* process has helped to restore your birthright as the unique, gifted, beautiful human being that you are.

Spiritual success is not about perfection, elevating off the couch, performing rituals, or meditating on a mountaintop. Immersing yourself in books, classes, and workshops is a wonderful way to learn, but they are only tools to inspire you to be the person you already are. You need not to travel abroad, join a convent, or check into another healing center. You need only to journey within. Whenever you are anxious or afraid, you acknowledge you are not alone, feel the presence of your higher power, and connect with your inner knowing. We learn to rely on this divine intelligence rather than on our own limited, ego-driven minds.

Through identifying the significant points in your life, you were able to connect the dots and see that a unique course was charted just for you. Forgiveness replaces your resentments with loving thoughts and feelings. It is exciting to start a new life, empowered by a healed past—the beginning of your journey. The stairway to heaven has no end. Continuing success means you maintain a daily commitment to learn, grow, and forgive so that you do not slide back into the maze. You can learn a new skill, but if you do not practice, you will not improve. The more you practice, the better you are. Make sure you stay out of the complacency trap and keep moving forward.

A *Course in Miracles* defines a miracle as a change in perception. Miracles happen when you see your past differently so that those experiences are used to fulfill your life's purpose—to love and be loved. A miracle also occurs when you change your perception about a current situation. All reactions originate first from your thoughts. If you have a negative thought, you will have a negative reaction. You can learn how to prevent most reactions by asking your spirit to help you perceive a situation differently. Bringing your spiritual awareness into any situation will allow you to see through the eyes of love rather than fear.

This concept might be difficult to grasp, but if you keep practicing, you will maintain a sense of serenity, regardless of your circumstances. For example, when you awaken and your mind begins to barrage you with the usual negative fears (money, time, problems at work and with family), ask for spiritual guidance to help you see each situation differently. Like a game of tennis, return the ball back across the net rather than holding on to it. With consistent practice, you will get better and better at rejecting unwanted thoughts.

When you are spiritually present, you recognize that your life has a plan. You simply prepare yourself and embrace the opportunities presented to you. You do not have to make anything happen; you need only do your part. Thankfully, I was blessed to have inner guidance long before realizing I was on a spiritual path. Divorced with a child at age eighteen, with no child support, employed as a waitress, I felt doomed to a life of limitation and lack. However, something inside told me that I had a purpose, and I trusted that message. While pursuing a high school diploma at night school, I took secretarial courses. Soon, a neighbor told me of a job at an adult education center, and that job led to a short-term secretarial career. When it was time to go to college, I was terrified of failing, but I enrolled nonetheless. Psychology was a natural fit. Drawn to people and their problems, I was a go-to for many of my classmates who needed to share their problems. My mother, the cheerleader, encouraged me every step of the way. As one door opened to another, I earned an undergraduate degree, then a master's degree, and went into private practice with a colleague. Soon after, I followed the advice of my mentor, who insisted I continue on for a doctorate degree. All of this would have been impossible without connecting to guidance that was beyond my own limited self-perception. I have cherished a fulfilling career that helps people to change their lives for the better.

My emotional and spiritual process also was a matter of connecting the dots. When I was listening to my intuition, I made good decisions. When I ignored the wise voice and exercised my willfulness, I made mistakes. When I learned why I made those mistakes, grew through my feelings, and forgave myself and others, I could see the value in all of my life's experiences—especially the failures. My biggest mistakes have become my greatest strengths.

You are here for a reason. When you stay emotionally connected and use the learn, grow, and forgive tools for navigating your way through the unforeseen roadblocks, nothing will stop you. You are already a success.

The More You Share, the More You Have

Spiritual success is being love. *A Course in Miracles* tells us the problem is not lack of love; love is always within us and all around us. We need not to search for love; instead, we "remove the blocks to love's awareness." Learning, growing, and forgiving is a process that removes these blocks. When healed, we no longer use anything to escape from our loneliness and misery. Since all relationships are designed to help us learn, grow, and forgive, when triggered, we use that as a signal to do more work. We are grateful that our relationships help us identify our wounds, and we are committed to healing them.

When you act from love, your fear-based emotions lose power over you. When we seek love, we do not find it; love finds us when we are loving. Some of us have used people and loved things rather than loving people and using things. When we love ourselves, we have something to share with others rather than being on the take. Loving ourselves means filling ourselves with all the spiritual nourishment we need. We can do this through prayer, meditation, relationships, culture, music, nature, or whatever inspires us. You already know what feeds your spirit—the things that you love.

A *Course in Miracles* tells us that "every encounter is a holy encounter" and that "love waits on welcome, not on time." It could be a brief encounter with a stranger or a deep encounter with a friend. When two hearts open to each another, love expands. You can choose to share and receive love with anyone who is willing—whenever and wherever. Our ego always wants us back in the maze. However, now, when you feel isolated or alone, you can open yourself to love wherever you are. You are the one in charge of you. The more you give, the more you receive. If someone does not want to connect, do not react—simply send love and move on.

By now, your jar should be full of red hearts. There is always someone who needs your love, and there never is a wrong time to show someone that you love them.

Now Is Always and Forever

Most of us complain that there is never enough time or that time goes by too fast. Lack of time is an illusion. When we stop procrastinating or filling up every minute of our day instead of pacing ourselves, there is always enough time. When we give the first few minutes of our morning to meditation, prayer, and reading, and end the day with thankfulness, we are bound to enjoy a more peaceful life. This morning nourishment gives us the grace to face with ease whatever comes to us. As we practice, we lose any tolerance for agitation, and when something is bothersome, we can quickly shift from fear into a learn, grow, forgive, miracle-minded consciousness.

When our day is devoted to a path of growth, we find that time has a different meaning. We leave early so that we are not agitated on the way to an appointment. Whether we are dining, working, or visiting a friend, we are satisfied, because we are fully present in those moments. When we have free time, we engage in a favorite hobby, check on a loved one, meditate, or just enjoy being alive. When the body can no longer serve the spirit, we graciously accept it is time to return home. We have made peace with whoever asks, knowing it is for them, not us, because we have already made peace with ourselves.

Josh was angry with his father and had not spoken to him for more than twenty years. His father was a religious man and very devoted to his family, but Josh had not recovered from his childhood wounds. Through learning, growing, and forgiving, Josh made peace with his past and decided to call his father. Overwhelmed, his elderly parent cried during the first part of the conversation. Over the next year, Josh and his father were able to have a relationship in the here-and-now and reunited as father and son. Shortly after that, Josh's father was diagnosed with terminal cancer, and Josh was at his side when he passed. He was sad to lose his newly found father but ever so grateful that he had made peace with this man who had participated in giving him the gift of life. His father's death helped him to realize the importance of loving a family member before the doors between two worlds had closed.

We are born with birth certificates but not death certificates. Our time here is unknown. Time helps us to remember that every moment of every day is a gift.

Money Flows Like the Ocean

Like the ocean, money has a natural ebb and flow. There are times of excess and times of reduction, but a good steward always has enough. Some people waste money without any regard for the inevitable shortages. Wise use of money means we balance saving, spending, paying bills, and sharing.

A Course in Miracles tells us, "To have all, give all to all." This teaches us to have a consciousness of abundance. Imagine that money comes in and out through an invisible pipeline. When we are generous—even if we feel poor—we are widening the channel to receive. If you are pondering whether to give a lower or higher amount, go higher; you are investing in your own prosperity. If you do not have money, share something else; it will come back tenfold or greater. I recently saw a homeless man gleefully flinging his food to an eager flock of pigeons. The childlike smile on his face filled my heart with a warmth that lasted all day.

When we deny lack, we stay in a state of trust. We know that as long as we are willing to show up, the opportunities to earn will present themselves. Fear cannot take hold in a consciousness of trust. Never be afraid to try something new. If the funds have diminished from one source, affirm that another door is opening.

Rather than obsessing about your bank account balance, turn your focus to what is all around you. Everywhere you look, there is an endless amount of life: land, trees, skies, stars, waterways, not to mention all of your personal belongings. Can you see a constant source of creation that makes your life better? Humans evolved from dwelling in caves and trees to living in elegant homes with appliances, comfortable furniture, electricity, plumbing, and other amenities. Even homeless people have found their way to success through creative thoughts, dreams, and gratitude. You can be thankful for your surroundings rather than focusing on what you do not have. *A Course in Miracles* teaches us that the only lack with which we need concern ourselves is the lack of creativity. Everything you see is a part of creation, and creation never ceases.

Jane, a divorced mother of two, was struggling financially. Her salary and tips at a coffee shop covered only her rent and utilities, with nothing left over. She knew she had to do something. Someone at her church suggested she start reading books on how to create prosperity. Jane learned that she could increase her wealth by tithing. She had read that every amount she gave would come back tenfold and started adding two extra dollars to the offering every Sunday. She was shocked to see that her tips suddenly increased ten to twenty dollars a week. The more her tips increased, the more she put in the offering.

Newly inspired, Jane did not stop there. She wanted to make something of herself, so she used her creativity to manifest that vision of success. She had always loved cooking, so with her meager savings, she decided to attend a cookie and cake decorating class. Jane loved her new hobby so much that she started baking homemade cookies, and she received accolades from those who enjoyed her beautiful creations.

Inspired, Jane decided to ask her boss if she could sell them at the coffee shop and split the profits. After sampling her mouth-watering cookies, he readily agreed. It did not take long for her beautifully decorated cookies to sell off the shelf. Jane hired a website designer, and now she has an internet business that keeps her busy full time. Within a year, Jane had to rent space in a commercial kitchen and hire two helpers to fill the long list of orders. When she replaced her fear of financial lack with tithing and her creative talent, prosperity found its way to her. We arrive here with nothing, and we leave with nothing; everything else is a gift.

Heaven Is Now

When I was about ten years old, a friend invited me to one of my first church services. Upon returning home, I asked my nonreligious mother if there was such a thing as hell. She told me that hell was a state of mind. "You have a choice," she said. "You can be in heaven, or you can be in hell." Though I intuitively knew what she meant, it took many years for me to understand her words of wisdom fully. When we live in a loving consciousness, our actions follow, and we have peace of mind—heaven. When we allow our minds to wallow in conflict, guilt, and turbulence, we are miserable—hell.

This first course in spirituality helped me to understand that I was the one responsible for my happiness. I could not blame a mean God for my woes in life. There are choices to be made; sometimes, they were good choices, and sometimes bad. I was the one responsible for my mistakes and the one responsible for correcting them, whenever possible. I had no control over unexpected misfortunes, but I *did* have control over my attitude about those disappointments. It was not until much later, when I became a student of *A Course in Miracles* that I learned how to choose between two states of mind: love or fear. Just as my mother taught me when I was ten years old: one is heaven, and one is hell.

Laugh until Your Belly Turns to Jelly

When nothing else works, there is one sure thing that will save you: laughter (especially laughing at yourself). A sense of humor is endearing and redeeming, and one of the most charming characteristics you can possess. Seeing through the eyes of humor allows you to transform any heavily felt situation into lighthearted fun. A friend told me how humor reframed his perception of his first AA meeting. A detached observer throughout the meeting, when he was about to leave, he was approached by a gentleman who asked him what he thought about the meeting.

He replied, "I thought they were a bunch of tap-dancing, fast-talking con artists."

To which the man replied, "Then you'll fit right in."

Able to use humor to cut through his defenses, my friend has been a solid member of AA for the past thirty years.

Laughter is also a balm for physical illness. Norman Cousins became famous for laughing his way out of sickness. After being diagnosed with a rare and fatal disease, he used television comedy and holistic healing to extend his life another twenty-five years.

You can turn any drama into comedy by using your creative thoughts to rewrite the tone of your story. Amidst doom and gloom, you can still feel your grief, but if you embrace it with humor, your sorrow will always have a silver lining.

The We Program

The most important part of spiritual success is what I like to call the "we program." When considering someone else's interests with your own best interests, you are in a win-win mind-set. Spiritual-mindedness means being service-minded rather than self-serving. We care as much about loved ones as ourselves. Most conflicts occur when people are self-absorbed and oblivious to the needs of others. We need not push too hard or exhaust ourselves by doing for others. Sharing can be as simple as yielding to a pedestrian or offering to help a friend or family member with a minor task. The more you give, the more love you feel.

George and Terry met as coworkers at a business at which George was a co-owner. George was in a relationship at the time, but when that relationship ended, George and Terry became lovers. They were together for seven years, and when the relationship lost its spark, they decided to stop the romantic part of their union. In spite of the breakup and the expected emotional upheavals, they maintained their connection, placing their friendship first. It was difficult staying close; sometimes, they did not speak for days, but both were secure that neither was abandoning the relationship. They overcame another challenge when George faced a termination with his business partner. Instead of collapsing under the stress and going their separate ways, George and Terry stuck it out and decided to open their own business.

As time went on, the two achieved an even closer friendship based on the trust that they could always count on being present for each other, no matter what. Several years after their relationship ended, George met someone, fell in love, and decided to marry. Because of the loving bond that Terry and George shared, Terry offered to officiate the wedding ceremony. Terry felt genuinely honored as the one who would bless the union of George and his spouse. Today, eight years later, Terry and George still are business partners with a bond as deep as ever.

This beautiful story is about how love remains when neither person walks away, and both allow the love to change form. Love does not die; it will fill any opening that is available. George and Terry kept their hearts open; thus, the love between them remained. Their suffering was minimal because they stayed connected. By caring about each other, they were able to make it through the transition from lovers back to friends, blessed to allow their love to remain. Love never dies; it remains ever ready to fill whatever opening is available.

Spiritual success is no different from any other form of success. The more you immerse yourself, the quicker you see results. Success does not mean perfection; it simply means you continue to learn, grow, and forgive so that you keep moving through any blockages.

We are here to sing, dance, and play on this beautiful merry-go-round called earth. The possibilities for loving encounters are endless; we could never indulge in all of the fun things to do. When we fall, we nurture the cuts and scrapes, and then use those experiences to help others. We live a plentiful mind-set, and abundance follows. We are committed to living, laughing, and sharing. We want to heal anything that stands in the way of those pleasures. We enjoy the love that we share as we watch our lives transform from a flickering candle into a radiant light.

Now is the time for you to realize that you are a success. Now is the time to feel the love that you are. Now is the time for you to recapture your dreams. Nothing can hold you back, as long as you continue to learn, grow, and forgive. Let your light shine. Let your love grow. Heaven is now; let it in. Never give up; never, never, never.

Daily Habits for Spiritual Success

1. Start your day with prayer and meditation. This need not be a lengthy process. Simply ask your higher power to guide you through the day and ask for help.

2. Every time you feel a reaction, promptly do your re-centering exercises. Face the demons of the past, but refuse to entertain them.

3. Remember to be grateful all day long; say, "Thank you," for the pleasant and the unpleasant. They both are designed to facilitate your process of learning, growing, and forgiving.

4. Make a point of connecting with a stranger every day. You do not have to make this happen; people will be put in your path. Once you get accustomed to looking someone in the eye, smiling, and sending them love, you will begin to see that you are surrounded by love most of the time. If someone does not respond, simply wish them well and move on.

5. Attempt to give a compliment to everyone you encounter; offer many compliments to those who are closest to you.

6. Be aware of your surroundings and the beauty that they hold. Never take the sun, moon, stars, and nature for granted. Everything around you serves to make your life better.

7. Think hard when taking risks; remember that the ego is in waiting. If you make a mistake, own it, fix it if possible, and refuse to dwell on it. This is a victory for the spirit and a loss for the ego.

8. Remember to go with the flow, allow things to come to you naturally, and let go of the things that are ready to leave you.

9. Remember the we program: considering another person's wants and needs with your own.

10. Quickly center and release any grievances that try to attach to you.

11. Smile until your cheeks hurt; allow your light to shine.

12. Say a prayer at night, giving thanks for each event of the day that blessed you and helped you to grow.

Conclusion

It is my deepest desire that you recapture your true self through *Learn, Grow, Forgive,* and that you are filled with new hope. As someone who has faced a great deal of pain, I understand the lasting effects of betrayals and other life tragedies. I know how hard it is to come out of the imaginary safety of an angry wall or invisible cave. It is natural to fear an unknown future that could be worse than your past. When I began to heal, my perception of my entire life began to improve as well. I found out that I was not a victim and that my life had a definite plan. I chose certain events before I was born so that I could evolve spiritually and offer hope to others. There is no doubt in my mind that I am fulfilling my life's purpose and that nothing ever happened to me that was not part of a divine plan to help me achieve that goal.

I know that you can achieve that same happiness and that you are worth the effort you put into loving yourself. No one can do it for you, and you can succeed. When you are willing to learn, grow, and forgive, there is nothing to lose but old baggage and memories that do not serve you. However, I promise you that if you are willing to learn about what happened to you and the effects those experiences had on you, you will grow from everything that life has dealt you. If you have the courage to face your past and accept who you are now, you will be able to receive the gift of forgiveness. Reaching the other side, you will be able to live life to its fullest and love in a way that you never imagined.

Invite the future in; allow your heart to open to all the love around you. That is where you will find what you've been missing and what you've needed all of your life: your very own soul. Never stop learning, growing, and forgiving. Never, never, never.

Appendix

Recommended Reading

Berne, Eric.1964. *Games People Play –The Basic Handbook of Transactional Analysis*. New York: Ballantine Books.

Ehrman, Max. 1935 *"Desiderata"* in *The Poems by Max Ehrmann*. Boston, MA. Bruce Humphries Publishing Company.

Foundation for Inner Peace. 1992. *A Course in Miracles*. Glen Allen, CA: The Foundation for Inner Peace.

Hay, Louise. 1994. *You Can Heal Your Life*. Carlsbad, CA: Hay House.

Hill, Napoleon. 1935. *Think and Grow Rich*. New York: The Penguin Group.

Kubler-Ross, Elizabeth, and David Kessler. 2000. Kessler, *Life Lessons: Two Experts on Death and Dying Teach Us About the Mysteries of Life*. New York, New York: Scribner Press.

Twelve-Step Programs

Alcoholics Anonymous

Adult Children of Alcoholics

Al-Anon

Overeaters Anonymous

Codependents Anonymous

Narcotics Anonymous

(There is a twelve-step program for every addiction; online meetings are available.)

A Course in Miracles Study Groups

The book is available online or in bookstores. There are study groups across the world.

Temple of the Universe

Located in Alachua, Florida, and operated by Michael Singer, author of *The Untethered Soul* and *The Surrender Experiment.*

Psychoanalytic Associations

American Psychoanalytic Association (APSA.ORG)

National Psychological Association for Psychoanalysis (NPAP.ORG)

New York Psychoanalytic Society and Institute (NYPSI.ORG)

Southeast Florida Association of Psychoanalytic Psychology (SEFAPP.ORG)

Most of these services are free of charge or provided on a love offering basis.

Free Bonus

Would you like more information on healing addiction?

Do you have trouble accessing your feelings?

Dr. Marks is offering a free meditation to help with this.

You can also watch her videos on addiction and her *Course in Miracles* classes.

Want more than a book?
You can sign up for an online course,
Exit the Maz: One Addiction, One Cause, One Cure,
to help accelerate your healing process.

For more information
and to access this bonus and videos,
please visit **www.drdonnamarks.com**

Printed in Great Britain
by Amazon

62001245R00129